# MANAGING WORK

# EFFECTIVE MANAGEMENT SKILLS

## MANAGING WORK

### JOHN SCOTT & ARTHUR ROCHESTER

Sphere/British Institute of Management

First published by
Sphere Books Ltd/BIM 1984

Typeset by H.M. Repros, Glasgow.

Printed and bound in Great Britain by
Cox & Wyman Ltd, Reading

# Contents

# Preliminaries

If there's anything a manager reckons he can manage standing on his head, it's work. In most cases, managers don't see its organisation, planning and control as a problem, compared with other aspects of management such as motivation and coping with the complexities of human nature, or understanding and manipulating the figures that represent the organisation's life-blood, money. Many have an innocent and quite unjustified belief in the uncomplicated nature of the things they have to get done. Perhaps this explains why so many managements don't work harder at managing their operations properly. When they run into difficulties, human cussedness or lack of resources usually get the blame. But often enough neither one nor the other are the real culprits. It's actually the fault of someone who's trying to get the wrong thing done, or trying to get it done the wrong way.

This book tries to show how this particular kind of problem can be tackled. It is one of a series that deals with the different angles of the manager's job. The first *What is a Manager?*, set the scene by analysing the basic features of organisations (i.e. the things that managers manage) to distinguish the manager's priorities in running them. It identified three priorities: the management of work, of people and of money. Each is the subject of one book in the series. The aim is to put together a view of the management job that is relevant to anyone from supervisors upwards, and to present it in down-to-earth accounts of the way good managers think and act.

One general point about the organisations whose work we're dealing with here. Most books about management seem mainly to be concerned with industrial and commercial organisations. Yet public bodies need managing no less than businesses — managing the work that goes on in the departments and agencies of national and local government, in state corporations, in every public service you can think of. It's certainly no less important a job for the sake of the country's economic health and its citizens' quality of life. But the sort of management it gets is generally far more feeble than the not-too-impressive management that much of the work of our business organisations receives. As far as this book is concerned (and the others in the series), we're dealing with what goes on in *any* managed organisation.

There's also a general point about the people who are managers — a practical problem to do with sex and English pronouns. Let's simply quote from the opening of *What is a Manager?*: a lot of managers are women, but to keep the style of writing simple you've got to choose your pronoun. Do you call a manager 'him' or 'her'? Our apologies to all the she-managers we might have insulted, but we've used 'him' throughout. It's a problem of language. Please don't take it as an attempt to cut half the human species out of management.

This book, like each of the others in the series, starts with a quiz. The idea is to get you to think what you *do* think about the issues we're going to take up, before we tell you what to think! No, seriously — there is something to be said for framing your own ideas first, so that you have a stand-point from which to judge the ideas we're putting forward. Each question gives you three answers to choose between, apart from the first which, as you'll see, is set up differently from the others. For the rest, it's a question of which answer you agree with most (although you may agree partly with all three, or wholly with none). Later you'll be able to look back to see if you'd still make each choice in the same way.

# Work-management quiz

1.  The 'work' that managers manage can be defined in various ways. Which, if any, of these definitions do you disagree with?
    a) Work is what people must do to earn a living.
    b) Work is something people need in order to maintain a sense of self-respect and purpose in their lives.
    c) Work is what organisations need done to fulfil their own purposes.

2.  Is it possible for a manager to *over*-manage the work he's responsible for getting done?
    a) Yes. If he's constantly deciding things his people could equally well decide for themselves, he's likely to get poorer results.
    b) Perhaps. If he's constantly trying to find out what is going on, it might suggest he doesn't trust his people.
    c) No. If anything goes wrong he'll have to take the blame, so it's only reasonable for him to control things as closely as he can.

3.  Different managers see the purpose of a business organisation's work in different ways. Which of these purposes is likely to lead to the most effective management decisions and actions?
    a) To provide high-quality goods and services.
    b) To create satisfied customers.
    c) To make good profits.

4.  There are many obvious differences between the ways that business organisations and public bodies operate. For their management, which of the following makes the biggest difference?
    a) The fact that businesses have to compete to survive, public bodies don't.
    b) The fact that businesses are profit-making, public bodies aren't.

c) The fact that a business has to sell its goods or services, a public body doesn't.

5. Which is the first question for a manager to consider when deciding how to divide up work between different people?
   a) How to enable the different activities to be properly coordinated.
   b) How to avoid conflicts of personality between the individuals concerned.
   c) How to match each person's work to his seniority and experience.

6. Who are the policy-makers in an organisation?
   a) In any organisation, policy is made solely by its top management.
   b) Managers at each level are the policy-makers for those at the next level below.
   c) Every manager makes policies for employees throughout the area he manages.

7. Should managers have job descriptions for their people's work?
   a) Yes — primarily to tell each person what tasks he must perform.
   b) Yes — primarily to let everyone know the boundaries within which each person has freedom to operate.
   c) No. They limit people's scope for using their initiative and for taking responsibility.

8. What is a manager actually doing when he establishes aims for the work he's responsible for?
   a) He is forecasting the results that are likely to come about.
   b) He is deciding what he and his people must and mustn't do.
   c) He is creating ideas about what he and his people might be able to achieve.

9. Which is the most important reason why a manager should plan?
   a) To protect himself against criticism by his superiors if things go wrong.

b) To try and foresee problems and decide what to do about them before they arise.
c) To enable him to know when things are off-course so that he can correct the situation.

10. Which managers should be involved in marketing?
   a) All managers, whether they're employed in businesses or in public service, because marketing is really the ultimate purpose of any managed organisation.
   b) Only managers in Sales or associated departments, because marketing is a highly specialised activity.
   c) Managers throughout any business organisation, because they're all dependent on the results the organisation achieves.

# 1. The four-letter word

Of course, we all know what work is. The general idea is that it is what 'workers' do. It involves being very obviously busy, usually in activities that are physically or mentally strenuous. The typical picture of the worker most people carry around in their heads is of someone wearing overalls or some other kind of working clothes, doing something that is probably rather tiresome and boring and that makes him sweaty and dirty, getting home exhausted and grumpy at the end of the day or the shift or however else the hours are arranged that he spends in the horrid activity. And he gets paid for it. It's a picture that's confirmed every time someone who's doing a job that's interesting and not conspicuously arduous is asked "D'you call that *work*?" — and the question makes him feel guilty. When you work, you're not supposed to enjoy what you're doing. You only do it for the money.

For most people in jobs, the picture is some way off the reality. But how *do* you define 'work'? There's a basic fallacy in almost any attempt to say what it is in simple terms. If you say "work is what you don't like doing but have got to do", you come up against people who actually get as much satisfaction out of the things they do in their jobs as they get from the way they spend their free time. If you say "work is something you've got to put effort into", you're ignoring all those people whose leisure activities demand much more energy that the work they're employed in. If you say "work is what you get paid to do" and you happen to be a married man with a wife at home, see what *she* thinks of that idea. Definitions like these have too many holes in them to be totally true. Some of the problem comes from conventional cartoon-type images of 'the worker' — either cloth-capped, scruffy, thick and idle, or cloth-capped, brawny, boldly facing the world and improbably holding a flag. Then the whole question gets converted into a class issue. This is the fix that a lot of trades union thinking has got into where there is a deep-seated habit of regarding work as something really done only by those at the shop-floor level of our organisations. The distinction that's commonly made between 'workers' and 'management' by union representatives and even by managements themselves, heaven help us, seems to imply that whatever management does, it doesn't do *real* work. The militant leftist will often defend this view by pointing out that the organisation couldn't exist without the fruits of its workers' labours. That's obvious. But it also suggests that the managers' activities aren't equally essential. Try putting *that* point to the hardworking, dedicated workers in a collapsing company where it's the failure of the managment to do *their* work properly that has led to the collapse.

The difficulty is really in trying to separate 'work' from any other kind of human activity. There can hardly be *any* activity that isn't work for some and a leisure interest for others — from the weekend archaeologist digging holes in the ground to the schoolboy computer fiend developing new programmes in his spare time. Even a game of tennis or football is a serious matter to the professional player.

It's a problem that's illustrated by the story of the artist who lived in a country cottage — a professional artist who lived off the sale of his pictures. Early one morning he had set up his easel on his lawn and was busy at his canvas when a gardener passed by on his way to work. "Must be nice to relax on a day like this" the gardener called. "I'm not relaxing — I'm working" replied the artist. The gardener snorted in disgust at the easy life some people had, and strode on towards the garden in which he was working that day. And all morning under the hot sun he toiled with fork and hoe. Passing the cottage on his way home to lunch, he saw the artist had left his easel and was busily weeding one of his flower beds. "Good to see you getting down to a spot of real work" called the gardener. "This isn't work", said the artist. "I'm relaxing".

In a primitive society there's a simple way of resolving the problem. They just don't try to make the distinction at all. The Yequana, a stone-age tribe living in the forests of Venezula, don't *have* a word for 'work'. For them, every activity has its own purpose in the fabric of their everyday lives, and they have never found any point in dividing it into separate lumps — 'this is work' — 'that is play'. They have no need for the pattern in our modern civilisations of strain and striving followed by exhausted 'relaxation', no need to compete with one another for food or possessions or to pressure their fellow human beings into doing things. Happiness is a normal condition of being alive and active. We might regret our long-passed loss of that Garden of Eden existence, but as members of the developed world we have to accept that for us work is a necessary idea. It has created too many material benefits for us to give it up now.

Perhaps the real problem for us in our society is that we try to be too simplistic in defining what we mean by 'work'. We look for a single all-purpose definition, and that's the fallacy. There isn't one. There are several.

To start with, the title of this book has already established one distinguishing feature of the kind of activity we're talking about. The 'work' that we're concerned with here is an activity that is *managed* in some way. That may beg the question of what 'managing' means when it's related to work. We'll come back to that. But there *is* one thing that it implies. If it's 'managed' the work has to be done in an *organisation* of some sort. True, there are a lot of people who do their work outside organisations — the self-employed window-cleaner or shop-keeper, the freelance journalist or management consultant. But for most people in Western civilisations, work is something done as an employee of an organisation.

Looked at in this way, there are at least three different meanings to the word:

## 1. The 'work' you do to earn a living
This makes the real point of work the money you get for doing it. It's the idea of the employment contract. The 'meaning' of work is in receiving pay for the hours you put into it and for accepting that you've got to obey orders. You're not free to choose what you do or how you do it. The activities may be monotonous or stressful, and you may have to put up with indignities and frustrations in doing them. You have to accept your boss's authority no matter what snobbery, arrogance or other absurdities he displays. In this sense, work may be truly 'what you don't like doing but have to do'.

But even pay-slaves can become willing to put their livelihoods at risk if the indignities become just too much to bear. Most of the nation found it difficult to comprehend why the workforce in a car factory that had been within a stones-throw of closure could strike for a month over a mere six minutes extra work the management were demanding at the beginning and end of each shift. This was the 'wash-up time' dispute in British Leyland. The popular idea was that militant unionists were at it again. The real cause of the trouble turned out to be not the extra minutes but the bullying, inconsiderate treatment the workforce was being subjected to by its managers. One of its members, no militant but a moderate, middle-of-the-road Labour supporter, cited a case of a worker with diarrhoea who asked his supervisor for a relief to take his place on the line for a couple of minutes. He was ordered to stay at his workplace. When he eventually could delay the demands of nature no longer, he was issued with a formal disciplinary letter the next day. ''There were endless examples of this sort of thing. They used to shout and swear and abuse people. There were threats to dismiss people, and all this

4

produced very real anxiety and a steady build-up of tension''. The demand for the extra minutes and the way it was presented to the workforce was simply the final straw on an already-overloaded camel.

To keep their jobs and their pay-packets, many people still accept treatment that was supposed to have disappeared with nineteenth century sweatshops. But it confirms them in their view that work is basically unpleasant and demeaning — something that no one in his right mind would do if he had any other option. And it makes some pretty powerful advertising for the left-wing militants' creed of 'workers' in eternal conflict with 'managers'.

## 2. The 'work' you need for self-respect and a sense of purpose

This way of looking at work raises the question of what people would do if they *didn't* have to earn a living. Most of us would still need something purposeful to occupy ourselves with rather than just sitting around. Take away *all* work, and most people's lives would fall apart leaving little more than meaningless bits of social relationships — which is the real problem for most of our vast army of unemployed.

This isn't saying that work is something everyone necessarily *wants* to do. The idea of work as satisfying a need for purpose and meaning in people's lives is much more complicated than that. *Some* work we may actually like doing — the parts of our jobs that we find intrinsically interesting or

5

rewarding as compared with other parts that are a grind: that's like the difference between your youngster's feelings' about the almighty boredom of helping mother peel the potatoes and the joy of making a whole apple pie 'all by myself'. With the potato-peeling kind of work, the point may be more to do with the satisfaction of having got it finished. Those are the nagging jobs we know we have to do but actually hate doing — like the fag of tidying cluttered cupboards or writing up a boring report, yawn, yawn — the motivation lies in working towards the sense of relief that we know we'll feel when we've got them out of the way. Even coping with the very hardness of hard work is something that most people can get a sense of achievement out of — in short bursts anyway.

Everyone needs some kind of pattern in their lives — some purposeful activity that shapes the way we use our time. And work is the main source of that pattern. A few can create one for themselves. But if most of us were left entirely to our own devices, we'd be hard pushed to continually find things to do that are worth doing. Much as we may grumble about work, we need the discipline of having to knuckle down and get on with a succession of given tasks. It's a discipline that answers a deep-felt desire in most people for order and regularity.

But the real point is the way most of us identify ourselves with our trade or occupation, and get a sense of what other people 'are' by finding out what sort of work they do. Beyond having to have an occupation to earn a living, and whether or not people actually enjoy what they do, for nearly all of us work is the stuff that makes sense of our lives. It creates a kind of purpose for living. If you doubt this, think of the effect of retirement. Many people who lack any other interest which can be turned into a purposeful post-retirement occupation, once they lose the pattern and purpose that their work gave their lives, are mentally finished — and soon physically finished too. They have nothing to live for.

Most people *want* to be fulfilled by the jobs they do, whether they're managers or 'workers'. Many do take considerable pride in their work, often in jobs that are classed as 'unskilled' by the organisations that employ them. Some years ago, someone who had himself been a civil servant and a journalist spent a couple of years as an ordinary worker in several different organisations. His account of his experiences told of the interest and effort he saw put into their jobs by a variety of people he worked with — unmotivated by their managers and often in spite of appallingly bad management.

6

There was Harry for example, an 'unskilled' worker in the maintenance department of a printing firm:

"Harry's energy was inexhaustible and he liked his work, particularly for the variety of challenges. While I was there he made two book-cases, burglar-proofed some windows, repaired a whole variety of mechanical breakdowns, fixed time-clocks vandalised by apprentices, mended electric motors, pumps, an arc light and a huge photogravure camera. In fact he turned his hand to any problem, often solving it with considerable ingenuity.

He was, like so many working people, basically technicate: he understood automatically the logic of a switch, a gear or an impeller. He saw nothing extraordinary in this: it was only part of a daily life that also included loading lorries, minding the central heating plant, shifting rubbish, sorting and weighing the blockmaker's offcuts, and acting as janitor.

Even so we were not regarded as skilled, and were paid accordingly. By what definition of skill could Harry's job be excluded from it?"

The manager who has a proper consideration for his people understands this meaning of work; he also understands the effort that his people are willing to put in if they *do* find a personal purpose in it beyond the wage packet. His management of them tries to allow them the dignity and self-respect that enables them to find a personal meaning in their jobs — a meaning that makes their work a little bit more than simply earning a living.

### 3. The 'work' an organisation needs done

In this sense the meaning of work is its physical end-result. It's defined by the purpose of the organisation: what does the organisation exist to *do?* All the real work that goes on inside it is in response to that question. Anything that's done that can't be related somehow to the question is mere foolishness.

For the manager this *ought* to be the primary meaning of the 'work' he manages. Good bosses tend to be tough but fair (which takes care of the first two meanings) and to keep their eye on the ball. And the ball is the required end-product of their people's work — the results of their activity that help the organisation satisfy its 'customers', whoever they are. The work may in fact be a long way upstream of the point where its eventual results flow into the world beyond — in purchasing or finance or administrative functions, say. But that only makes it the more necessary for its managers to make the connection between it and the organisation's prime purpose a real one.

There have been frequent attempts to explain the mysterious ability of many foreign-owned factories in Britain to get higher productivity and better workmanship from their local workforces than comparable British firms. Many are Japanese-run, but not all. Germans, Swedes and French have been equally successful. Some people think the explanation must be some superior gimmicks of 'motivation' — like early morning meetings of an entire workforce or the introduction of Quality Circles or managers wearing the same uniform as their workers and eating in the same canteens.

But when you talk to the workers themselves in those factories, things like these come across as incidentals to the main point: it's that their bosses care passionately about the products they make. The quality common to every successful manger is *a painstaking attention to the products of his own patch of responsibility.* There is a fundamental sense of rightness about working hard and to high standards for a bloke like that.

Basics often look childishly simple. That doesn't prevent them from being lastingly right — and frequently forgotten. Konosuke Matsushita, the creator of one of Japan's greatest electrical firms, set out to achieve four simple goals:
- 'make quality products'
- 'constantly strive to improve'
- 'take care of regular customers'
- 'maintain good relations with suppliers'

Each is a goal for the work done by the people in this organisation, a goal that puts the emphasis on the quality of the end-result in terms of products and relationships with people in the market place.

Of course there are British firms whose managements display the same concern — and with the same kinds of result. There's the example of a manufacturer of overcoats in the north of England — an unremarkable firm, except for its sense of purpose. And its profits. Every morning at 11 am everyone who wants to troops along to the design office to look at yesterday's production, to try it on, pull it apart, examine it, discuss it, come up with ideas about it. The boss is there, the despatch manager, production supervisors and workers, designers. In fact that design office is the heart of the business. There's no social chit-chat about football or families — all that anyone talks about with his boss and his colleagues is overcoats. No one would have it otherwise. The firm happens to sell rather a lot of overcoats to the Russians.

The point holds good for any kind of organisation, business or public body. Whether its a school or hospital, bank or hotel, local garage or international construction company, its success and its reputation with its public depend on its managers' dedication to high standards in the *work* they are resonsible for, the work that contributes to their organisation's purpose.

If you're a good manager, you've found a way of combining these three meanings of work in the activities of every one of your people. Their jobs give them both a living *and* a sense of purpose and self-respect, and all the while they're getting done the things your organisation needs done. This isn't an impossibly idealistic idea of what work ought to be. Every trade, every industry, every arm of public service contains a few examples of organisations — or parts of organisations — whose managers succeed quietly and persistently in achieving the trick. But the sad truth is that organisations like this are still only a small minority.

For one thing, there's a lot of ape-work around in our organisations — perhaps in yours. Many, many jobs are filled with mechanical, routinized activities in which people are used as 'hands' rather than brains. In the past the largest mass of them was on the noisy production lines of huge factories. Now their location is increasingly moving to the quiet, tidy offices of our computer-operated future. Work doesn't add anything to people's sense of personal value simply because it's done in pleasant surroundings. True, the jobs provide them with a living and are contributing to their organisations' end-products. But if you're like most other managers in this situation, you've long ago given up any attempt to arrange the work you're in charge of so that your people can find some sense of personal satisfaction in doing it — if indeed you ever started to consider the point. Yet the continual stream of demands for your time and attention includes many problems that wouldn't *be* problems if your people felt more personal involvement in what they're being asked to do. Work that is meaningless for the people doing it is inevitably difficult to manage — and impossible to manage *well*.

Work that is pointless for the organisation itself is even worse. And a lot of work that goes on in our organisations is precisely that. It provides pay. Often that is all it provides. The people doing it can't kid themselves that it gives *them* a sense of purpose and personal worth. And it damages the organisations that employ them to do it because it wastes valuable resources — resources that could have been used to contribute to those organisations' purpose in society. Eventually society itself is the loser.

Such make-work jobs exist in their hundreds of thousands. The 'job' of the fitter's mate is one example. A few years ago there were reckoned to be half a million people doing it — unskilled men in deadend jobs who spend several hours of every day waiting for the craftsman to give them something to do. The real purpose of the job is to add to the craftsman's status and prestige. "Quite often," said one, "it seems a long day. You go home feeling a bloody sight more tired than if you'd done a good day's work. There isn't a chance of getting out of it".

It's the problem of those *in* jobs who are either under-employed or mis-employed. You find them in banks and insurance companies, on construction sites and in production plants, in the offices of local government and government departments. Management jobs aren't immune either. There's an office in a major airline that has a plate on the door saying 'Manager Nil Spares'. If you ask the man sitting behind the door what sort of work he does he'll explain that he's there to deal with situations where spares are needed but there are none of that particular item in the airline's stores. You might suppose that means he arranges to get the spares quick sharp. Not a bit of it — there's *another* department to do that. He's there to 'manage the problem'. Whatever that might mean, he has a whole team of staff to help him do it! Make-work jobs are plentiful in management as well as on the shop floor.

How do such jobs ever come into existence? Very often, it seems, as a result of some senior manager's bright ideas that don't connect up with the real need for work in his organisation. Senior people often display a shocking ignorance about what really goes on down in the engine-room. Sometimes jobs are invented simply to create an illusion of organisational tidyness, at other times to cope with problems that are actually being caused by poor management. Perhaps the work in them *does* need to stave off total chaos — but should it have become necessary in the first place?

# The four-letter word

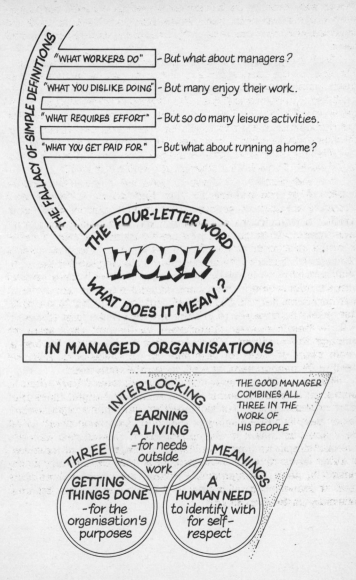

THE FALLACY OF SIMPLE DEFINITIONS

"WHAT WORKERS DO" – But what about managers?

"WHAT YOU DISLIKE DOING" – But many enjoy their work.

"WHAT REQUIRES EFFORT" – But so do many leisure activities.

"WHAT YOU GET PAID FOR" – But what about running a home?

THE FOUR-LETTER WORD
WORK
WHAT DOES IT MEAN?

IN MANAGED ORGANISATIONS

INTERLOCKING
THREE
MEANINGS

EARNING A LIVING – for needs outside work

GETTING THINGS DONE – for the organisation's purposes

A HUMAN NEED to identify with for self-respect

THE GOOD MANAGER COMBINES ALL THREE IN THE WORK OF HIS PEOPLE

# 2. Does work need managing?

You are a manager. Whether you're actually called a manager or supervisor or section leader or whatever, you've got the job of getting work done by other people. That's the basic definition of what 'managing' means. But do they really need you to be there telling them what to do and how to do it? It's a reasonable question to ask.

Most people aren't stupid. They manage somehow to cope for themselves with the job of living in our complicated world. For instance, if you happen to be a man with a wife and family at home, think of the job *she* handles, and without any manager to tell her how. Balancing the budget? That's what she's doing when she announces she's having the house repainted and her new fridge will have to wait. Keeping the junior staff happy? That gets her carefully equating one's safari park plus two Cokes with the other's circus plus Giant Zoom Wonder Ice. Planning? That's her decision on Greece this year instead of the Costa Brava *again*. Problem solving? That's her finding somewhere for Grandad to live because he can't cope on his own any longer. Delegation? Any mother who's got her offspring to do the ironing must know a thing or two about that. What's she doing if she isn't managing her work herself? Of course, some women are rotten at these things — just as most men are rotten at managing other people's work. But folk in general do passably well at deciding things for themselves in their private lives.

So why do they need a manager to make decisions for them when they're at work? After all, whether the folk are you or whether they're the people you manage, you've all got approximately the same amount of grey matter upstairs. If *they've* been in the job for a while, surely they don't need *you* coming along telling them how to do things? They're experienced. They've got nous. They can work it out for themselves. True, that doesn't stop them doing something stupid now and again — but they can usually see that for themselves afterwards. And do *you* never do anything daft yourself?

A manager wastes his own time when he gives instructions about things his people are equally capable of doing for themselves. He makes a fool of himself when he 'manages' things his people understand better than he does. But that is precisely the folly many managers regularly commit. They act like a collection of amateur art critics telling a professional painter how to put paint on a canvas. You can find such management fools at all levels:

— a Board sets a completion date or a budget for a

14

project that the managers who'll be running it know hasn't a chance in hell of being met.

— an executive decides on a system change that the people who'll have to work it know is going to be wasteful and inefficient.

— a sales manager insists a salesman sells to a customer in a way the salesman knows from experience doesn't work with that particular customer.

— a production supervisor gives his workers a long list of detailed instructions for a job they could work out better for themselves if only he told them what was wanted.

If you happen to think such things don't go on, just take a few examples. Someone who had had a job as a stock-controller in a London store described the experience of working for fools:

"The frustration of being treated as an imbecile beggars description. All the people I worked with could have performed their tasks blindfolded, but management had to tell them how to do each one. The irony was that management had no idea even how to start on these tasks. We could and did do them better and faster on the rare occasions we were left on our own".

A management consultant described how he solved a problem with a major item of processing plant in one of his client companies:

"Both its management and a team of experts they had brought in failed to solve the problem. Eventually it was decided that I should try. Next morning I introduced myself to the operator, explained the problem and asked him if he had any ideas. He grinned and told me I was the first person to make this kind of approach. As I had done him the courtesy of asking his help, he proposed to tell me the answer, which he did in the main essentials in ten minutes. We had ironed out all the details by lunchtime".

A skilled gardener described the sense of futility and waste in working for fools. In this case they were officers in a municipal Parks Department:

"Most of the time the management here seem more concerned to split us up than to get the work done. With a really big job — planting the long flowerbed or raking the field for instance — they'll always choose to have one person slogging away on his own, day in day out for a fortnight. That's always a bad way to organise it. Five of us could finish it off in a day and a half.

Our work never seems to envisage the park as a whole, or to make sense of the different methods of tending it through the seasons. Management gives us each little job in isolation, never telling us what we'll be told to do next. Often we know that means we're doing the job wrong. For instance, we're never told what's going to be planted in a flowerbed we're preparing. Even when we can see something that needs doing right away, we're never allowed any part in deciding when to do it or how — even down in petty details like which end to start sweeping a path''.

Management idiocies like that don't only frustrate almost past endurance the people being 'managed'. This last lot of official amateurs were also wasting the public money spent on the work they were 'managing'. And it's more than likely their parks provided less pleasure to the public than the gardeners could have managed by themselves at less cost. That isn't management. That's just interference.

And yet presumably none of these managers were stupid as *people*, whatever the stupidity of their management. On things they knew about and understood, they were probably as smart as anyone. Maybe it's often the fault of the 'system'. But a manager can often get himself into this fix without any help. How does he do it?

## 1. He's got the responsibility.
But he confuses that with trying to decide everything himself. He hasn't learned to trust the competence and interest of his people. Of course he has to know what his people *are* competent to work out for themselves, but how can he find that out if he never lets them decide anything? Do that, and it's more than likely they'll turn out to be better at some things than *he* is.

If you go on treating people as backward children who don't know when to come in out of the rain, they'll get into the habit of standing out there until they're told to come in. They'll do the things you tell them, even when they know they're *not* necessary. They'll leave things undone you haven't told them to do, even though they can see they *are* necessary. And they'll do things badly because they're not interested in the way they do them any more. To keep your people's interest alive in the work *you're* responsible for, you've got to give *them* responsibility too.

## 2. He's got the authority.

And maybe he feels that gives him free license to behave like a pocket Hitler. Given authority over other people, a lot of managers and supervisors make themselves quite ridiculous in the way they throw their weight around. Perhaps it's not altogether their fault. It might be an ego-defence against their fear or feeling personally insignificant. Or maybe their own bosses are putting them under pressure the same way. Funnily enough, when a manager like that is with *his* boss, he's often excessively deferential. He wants recognition for himself, not for his people. And he feels threatened if his people *do* turn out to be better than he is at anything he considers important (even if it's nothing more than deciding which end to start sweeping a path).

## 3. He's got the habit.

He's so used to giving petty instructions to people, he has never stopped to think that they could work out better instructions for themselves if he told them what was wanted and why. But he can't do that because he has always looked at work piecemeal — as a great pile of detailed things to do. He's never developed the organising skill of sorting the detail out into separate complete tasks. If he did so, he could give his instructions on what's needed more simply and clearly. *That* can become a habit too — and a more useful management habit than fiddling around unnecessarily with the nuts and bolts of the work. But there's never been anything to force him to do it — or anyone. His bosses don't push him to try. Perhaps they don't do it themselves either, so it's a chain reaction down through the organisation. Too many managers continue to manage by habit — and bad habit at that.

If you're managing things that don't need managing, you're probably making a mess of them. There *is* a management job to do, but it doesn't consist of being an interfering busybody. Of course, if you're determined to go on being one and your boss lets you, there's often no one else about to stop you. But consider the damage that sort of behaviour causes for the organisation itself — not just to the morale of your people. The silliest and most unnecessary problems that an organisation can suffer from are the self-inflicted wounds caused by its managers deciding things they don't properly understand and that don't need their decisions.

Now it's very possible that all this puzzles you. You might be one of those many, many managers and supervisors who are amazed that there are people in management jobs who've got *time* for such nonsense. Their own jobs are quite busy enough without taking on any more managing then they've got to do anyway. If your job is like that, you're continually like a cook trying to prepare a full breakfast by himself: you've got the bacon under the grill and the eggs in the frying pan and the bread in the toaster, plus the tea you're brewing and the plates you're warming. And in *your* kitchen at the same time you're also making the marmalade, churning the butter and baking the bread for tomorrow's breakfast — and trying to remember the toaster is unreliable and the grill has a habit of catching fire if it isn't constantly watched. The management job is often incredibly active. It's filled with great quantities of work done at top speed and you're continually being interrupted, never getting time to settle to one thing before something else crops up.

In an organisation of any size, the real problem of managing work is its sheer complexity. To avoid missing anything important you've got to have your wits about you, trying to keep everything in view that might require you to take decisions on the work of your people. And not only the work. You've also got your people themselves to consider and the way the costs of your operation are made up. Beyond that, there's the way the work *you're* responsible for affects the work going on elsewhere — the work *other* managers are responsible for. To manage work well, you can't let anything that's important about it slip out of sight. Put like that, the problem sounds impossible. In practice it's not.

If the whole organisation is properly **coordinated,** the impossible becomes perfectly possible without everyone getting their knickers in a twist. Managers and supervisors have efficient methods of linking this work here to that work there and yet other work somewhere else... they've got systems that eventually encompass nearly all the work that anyone is doing anywhere in the whole pile of activity. In a small team that operates together, there's no excuse for coordination being a problem. The team members can sort most of it out themselves. But it's different when the tasks that have to be linked up are going on in different places and at different times, and when the people doing them can't see for themselves how others' tasks are being affected by the way they're doing their own. That's where managers earn their keep.

The really big problems of coordination come about when the tasks are not only separated in space and time, but also require different knowledge and skills. Then the people doing them can't understand the difficulties they are causing each other, even if they're told about them. Usually they don't want to know. It's not only a case of, say, the shop floor workers and supervisors not understanding a production control clerk's difficulties in chasing up a late order or a salesman's difficulties in explaining it to the customer. It's also when the Production Director isn't interested in the headaches his supervisors are battling with, and the Sales Manager can't see the connection with the poor results of his sales force. In an organisation, everyone is in the same boat, never mind which bit of it they're working on. Good coordination gets everyone rowing the boat in the same direction.

To coordinate work properly, you have to prepare your methods in advance. That entails knowing what kinds of coordination *can* be settled in advance. Some of it can't be. In a manufacturing business for instance, managers know what work is involved in getting its supplies of materials and parts; they know what work goes on in the factory to process the supplies into finished products; they know what work is required to sell them. So they *ought* to know what's needed is coordinate all that work. There are many *regular* and *predictable* needs for coordination. That's basic and obvious.

But there are also things they can't coordinate in advance. They don't know when a supplier is going to let them down, or when a vital piece of factory plant is going to develop a fault, or when a big customer is going to take his business elsewhere. Any one of them might require extra work from everyone to cope with the emergency — and that will need coordination too. But the need for it is *irregular* and *unpredictable*. No one can be sure exactly what will need to be done when it happens.

The basic idea is to get all the regular and predictable needs for coordination sewn up as well as they possibly can be. If that's been done, the emergencies are usually easier to handle. Managers have two main ways of doing it — they *structure* the work and they have *routines* for getting it done.


# A. Structure

This is the organisation's way of dividing up the work into jobs for its people and groups to do. It's the rule-book that's

supposed to settle any question of the who-does-what variety.

But the way the division is done also determines how much coordination is needed. Take a very simple example — two people decorating a room. Let's call them Andy and Bill, and let's suppose each can't see what the other is doing. They have to coordinate their tasks by talking to each other. They have four things to do altogether:

— strip the old wallpaper
— paint the ceiling
— paint the woodwork
— paper the walls.

Let's also suppose each of those tasks has to be given to one or the other of them.

One way of structuring the work might be this:

| Andy | Bill |
|------|------|
| — strip the wallpaper<br>— paint the ceiling | — paper the walls<br>— paint the woodwork |

The coordination needed between them is minimal. Assuming the ceiling has to be painted before the papering begins, it's just a question of Andy saying when he's finished so that Bill knows when he can start. One simple act of coordination that should be easy enough to get right.

But suppose the structure is this:

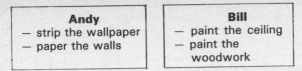

| **Andy** | **Bill** |
|---|---|
| — strip the wallpaper | — paint the ceiling |
| — paper the walls | — paint the woodwork |

Now there's a lot more coordination involved. This way it's possible for Andy to do his stripping while Bill does the ceiling — but they've got to pass messages to avoid getting in each other's way. Let's also suppose that Andy has to finish the papering before Bill starts on the woodwork. If Andy can work fast enough, he might manage that. They'll each need to know how the other is getting on so they can match their working speeds. There's got to be a lot more message-passing. But they'll probably finish quicker — and if Andy is the wallpaper expert and Bill is a dab hand at painting, they'll get a better result. If they don't have any coordination problems.

Every bit of an organisation's structure involves this kind of trade-off of advantages and disadvantages. On the one hand it may be more efficient to give each person in your group a collection of similar tasks. On the other hand, it may be less efficient if that makes it more difficult to coordinate — whether the coordination is between your people themselves, or between your whole group and groups elsewhere in the organisation. You can't simply look at each job to see if its work can be efficiently done. You also have to look at all the jobs to see if it's possible to coordinate the work properly when it's split up that way.

This division of work in an organisation is usually shown in a box-and-line diagram like this:

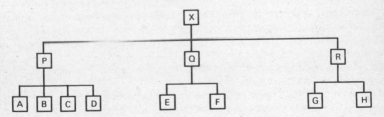

In most organisations the picture is much more complicated of course. This one might represent the way one area of work is structured. But it will do to show something else about the coordination that's involved in organisation structures.

Each box is a form of the 'Andy' and 'Bill' boxes you've just been looking at, but with many more tasks in it. It represents someone's job in the organisation. The P-Q-R jobs are the section leaders'. They include tasks of managing the people below them — including coordinating their work. The X job is a supervisor's who has to see that all the work is properly coordinated.

The lines show which jobs are supposed to be more closely connected. For instance, the A-B-C-D jobs are more closely coordinated with each other than they are with any of the other jobs at that level. (Whether they actually *need* that closer coordination is a question we'll come to in a moment.) The simple fact that they all head in to P makes it easier to coordinate what the four people are doing. With only four of them, they themselves can probably do most of the coordinating without P getting involved, but he's there if they can't.

Suppose coordination problems crop up. What the structure itself determines is the *number* of people who might be involved. If the coordination of A's and B's work causes a problem and they can't agree how to sort it out, P will do that for them. Just three people are involved. The management chain is a short one. But if (say) the coordination of A's and E's work causes a problem and they can't agree, it's going to involve both P and Q — and if *they* can't agree X as well. There's a longer management chain that drags five people into the problem.

Now perhaps you can see the implications of this. Suppose the work in the A-B-C-D jobs doesn't connect all that closely. But also suppose that some of their work *does* need to be closely coordinated with what the people in the E-F and G-H jobs are doing. The whole lot of them, including P-Q-R *and* X, are constantly going to be busy making decisions on coordination problems at the bottom level. The long management chains are constantly active. A problem that, given a different structure, would involve only one section will need everyone to get involved.

If the structure of a whole organisation is in this sort of mess, the signs are usually obvious:

— many people have a 'multiple boss' problem. That's when a person finds himself regularly getting instructions from several people, not just from the one who's supposed to be his boss. And the different things they tell him to do will often conflict.

— managers are spending too much time in ad hoc meetings to sort out regular, predictable problems. The meetings may have too many people present to be effective. They're all there trying to overcome coordination difficulties that the structure itself has created. The organisation is like a house with a hotplate in the kitchen, the cooker in the living room, the kettle in the bathroom and the fridge in the bedroom. So the cooks have to have constant meetings to get the cooking done.

— if you're in a junior position, you can't get more senior people to listen to your problems. They're battling with all the difficulties upstairs that stem from bad coordination downstairs. The structure is creating so many cock-ups, they simply can't stop problem-solving to see what's causing the problems. (It's also true that big shots tend to get sniffy if they're asked to look into what they regard as little-shot details. But bad coordination on a grand scale usually stems from bad organisation of the detail.)

— you're all drowning in the floods of information you're given in an attempt to coordinate what everyone is doing.

— there are attempts to control everyone down to the smallest details of their work. Systems have to be immensely complicated. The more complicated they are, the more likely it is that they'll go wrong.

If the whole organisation is being crippled by problems like these that's a job for the top people to tackle. The supervisor can hardly be expected to do it. But the same sorts of problems can happen within a department or section, and that's something that managers at the lower levels *can* do something about. Later in the book we'll look at practical things you can do to make sure that the bit of the organisation *you're* responsible for is properly structured.

Structure is the skeleton of the organisation. If it's bones are misshapen or misplaced, the organisational body can hardly work properly. But getting its structure right isn't enough. It also needs muscles and nerves — the routines that enable it to run. Nothing can operate at all without them. Nothing can operate efficiently unless the routines themselves are efficient.

# B. Routines

They way you get dressed in the morning is a routine — a series of automatic actions. Once you've decided which clothes to put on, there's no need to think what you do next at any point. Action by action, the only question is how you're performing each one. *You don't have to think to coordinate the actions.* That's what a routine does for you.

Routines are absolutely essential in any organisation — they're the only way it can cope efficiently with the vast mass of activities that need coordinating. Many of them are standard practice throughout the whole organisation. They are enforced by the policies of its top management, or are created by its systems of purchasing and stock control, work programming,

financial management, personnel administration and so on. But the smaller routines are important too: the methods you use to organise the work in your area, the procedures your people follow in doing it, the systems by which you keep yourself informed about progress. Besides creating your own routines, you've also got a part to play in maintaining the big routines. A whole system can be impaired by bits of it that are being worked in a sloppy, undisciplined way.

Of course, many routines are machine-operated and reduce the human element to a very small role. Work procedures are automated. Information processing is computerised. But this increases the importance of the people-operated bits that are left in those systems. And however far it goes, there always will be a need for human systems of work. In fact when a procedure is properly designed, it often turns out to be simpler and more cost-effective to have people operating it rather than going to all the expense of getting complicated equipment to do the job.

For you as a manager there's a simple point in devising a routine for anything that can be effectively run that way. It reduces the number of things you've got to make decisions about to more manageable proportions. That leaves you better placed to cope with all the coordination needs that *can't* be systematised. You use your time more efficiently and get your work done better and faster — more horsepower and less exhaust, as the saying goes.

But this doesn't make routines the answer to every managerial problem. If they're poor routines, they can actually *cause* inefficiency:

> — they can get people doing useless work. That's the sort of system by which someone toils to produce for a manager some weekly figures that he never uses. Nor did the manager before him. It was the manager two before *him* who originally needed them. Once. But the system he set up has continued running ever since. Before you introduce a routine like that, ask yourself whether what it's to do will still need doing in two months' time.

> — they can be unnecessary — imposing standardisation on something better left to personal judgement. A routine that exists merely to satisfy a manager's craving for uniformity uses people badly. It removes purpose and interest from their work. A gardener won't feel any less frustrated if it's a system rather than a manager that tells him which end of the path to start sweeping.

> — they can waste time even when some sort of routine *is* necessary for the work. That's the system that is badly designed. It gets people doing simple things in complicated ways — like setting up a major constructional exercise to build molehills. For example, many a Management by Objectives scheme is far too involved for what it's attempting to do. The managers running it get so wrapped up in its technical details they lose sight of the point of it all. Systems for people to follow need to be engineered on the KISS principle: Keep It Simple, Stupid!

> — they can fail to allow for exceptions to the rule. Where there's a system, it's sometimes difficult to stop things

getting into it that *can't* be treated by routine. You might be tempted to extend it to cope with those special situations. Resist the temptation. It makes it too complicated for everything *else* that goes through the system: remember the KISS principle. Accept that some things don't fit the system, and design it so they'll get noticed early.

But if things like these do happen with poor management, they don't prove that routines are unnecessary. The biggest problems are those caused by *not* having systems where systems are essential. A retired manager gave a detailed account of what went on in one company — a small engineering firm. It shows vividly what happens when systems are inadequate and badly run.

To keep himself occupied, and out of curiosity about the poor performance of many British organisations, he had taken on the job of progress chaser in the firm. On his first day he started trying to discover what parts were needed by the factory for urgent orders from customers. The story began in the Chairman's office:

> "The Chairman had ready a sheet of paper on which he personally had pencilled the products most urgently needed to satisfy customer orders, and the part numbers of the parts delaying their completion. There was no priority of urgency, no quantities, no indication of whether a part was made in the factory or bought from suppliers. I asked him none of these questions. I wanted the opportunity to dig the information out myself to learn how the place functioned."

He next found the stock control clerk:

> Together we tried to identify the exact position of each part on my list: the batch sizes of the products it was needed for; what had already been issued to the factory; whether the part was bought in — and if so, the purchase order number, date and supplier; if it was made in the firm, its factory order number."

The stock control records were in a mess — unreliable and incomplete. So after an hour and a half he gave up and went in search of the works foreman:

> "I learned that the Chairman's list was 'a lot of old cock'. I folded the list and put it in my pocket. I got from the foreman a list of products that the Chairman and Works Manager had been nagging him for to satisfy complaining

customers. I asked him to make a list of the parts he needed for the products he had listed.''

Then to find out which orders were actually outstanding, he asked the typist who kept the customer sales order files for help. But with no reliable record system, this was a forlorn hope:

''It was not possible to deduce which of the customers' orders had been partly or completely fulfilled. Some were with the receptionist/typist who did the invoices, or with the despatch department, or with the filing clerk — who didn't actually file them. She merely brought them back for filing.''

After lunch, the Works Manager:

''I stood over him while he produced a list of parts showing the priority of demands. Back to the foreman. He immediately flared up — the list wasn't a bit like the one he had prepared for me. I told him we would work to the Works Manager's list. Taking several items that were common to both lists, we extracted a number of parts that were holding up production. They were all bought from suppliers''.

So off to see the buyer:

''He at once claimed they were not short, that deliveries had been made and that the Works didn't know what it was talking about. Despite this, he promptly added he would chase the suppliers himself. I pointed out that stock control's records of his purchases could not be relied on. He at once claimed they were useless, but in the next breath admitted that he bought according to those records. What record could I go by? The purchase order copies of course. 'Let me see them' I asked. They were being collated (nice word, that)''.

Threats finally produced information of a sort, and he began phoning suppliers. What floated up to the surface from this stirring was remarkable. He was taken aback by the attitudes and inefficiency of the suppliers, most of whom seemed to be in no better shape than his own firm was.

His success in shocking the suppliers into hurried activity led to his being pressed to take the job of General Manager, three days after joining. He then proceeded to install what the firm desperately needed: efficient, reliable routines to coordinate purchasing, stock control, production scheduling and sales administration. That wasn't the whole story. There were other aspects of the firm's management that had to be sorted out too

— including the morale of its workforce and the effectiveness of its financial controls.

But this goes far enough to make the point about routines. It illustrates the messes that fester down below when a management doesn't realise the importance of systems, can't see where they're needed, can't design them, and can't run them with the necessary degree of discipline. Later on we'll talk about the techniques and skills that every manager needs — whatever his level — to ensure that whatever he is responsible for is run by system, not by chaotic and wasteful urgency.

At this point, let's stop and see where all this is getting us. The real problem of managing work in an organisation is its complexity, we've said. It's not that the work in each job is terribly complex (it *might* be, but that's not the point). It's that when you have a lot of different work going on in interlocking jobs, it gets very difficult to see how it all fits together — the way in which each bit or work might affect other bits.

This shouldn't be surprising. After all, that's exactly what happens inside a computer. The whole of its enormously complicated activity is built up of one tiny feature: whether, at a precise time and place in an electronic circuit, the electrical charge is positive or negative — does it say 'yes' or 'no'? But take that tiny feature and repeat it in a vast number of precise times and places throughout the system, and you get incredibly complex relationships between all those tiny electrical charges. It's more or less the same inside a big organisation. The difference is that each person in it is doing a much wider range of things than each yes/no point in a computer does.

To fit together all the bits of work in the various jobs, we've said they have to be coordinated somehow. And the basic way an organisation enables this to happen is by its structure — the way the work is split up into divisions, departments and sections. This is what decides where the coordination links are needed. A good structure is simply one in which it's easier to maintain the links: fewer of them are needed, and fewer people are involved in each one. A bad structure makes the links too complicated to manage efficiently.

Finally there are the routines — the methods used to provide the regular coordination that's needed between the jobs and the sections and the departments. They are the links to deal with anything that's *predictable*. You can predict a lot of things to do with physical work — like the way the delivery of materials affects what the people and machines in a factory can actually make. You can also predict many things to do with information

— like the way the information you've got about stocks and production affects the information you can give to customers. The systems that make connections like these are vital to all the work that's done in an organisation.

The point of having a routine for anything you know you've regularly got to get done is that it saves *your* time and everyone *else's* who's involved. The work is done faster and more efficiently. Whether you're the chief executive or a section-leader, you've got a responsibility to devise good systems for yourself and the people you manage. You've also got a responsibility for the parts that you run of the bigger systems in the organisation — to see that your bit is operated in a well-disciplined way.

What this leaves out, of course, are all the *unpredictable* things that have to be managed. In fact routines and procedures are often more the province of administration than of management. That doesn't deny that managers need some administrative ability for the sake of their systems. But the manager really comes into his own when systems can't cope. They can't do everything. In the work of an organisation, there are always things happening that lie beyond their reach.

That's where the manager has to make *decisions* — every manager, and all his people too.

## C. Decisions

Decisions are needed whenever a routine doesn't tell you *exactly* what to do. The systems you work within influence your decisions, certainly — particularly the bigger ones you take. They *ought* to help your decision-making:

> — they mark out the area of freedom you've got — what you can and can't decide for yourself. That enables you to act with more certainty in the decision you do take. But bounds ought occasionally to be overstepped when something happens that the system-makers didn't foresee. If a machine breaks down at a vital moment and you know for certain how to cure it, you could be doing the organisation a favour if you don't wait the half-hour the system takes to get an engineer. But you need to know if your boss would call that 'using your initiative' or 'stepping out of line'.
>
> — they often show you when there's a decision to be

made. Perhaps not actually *tell* you, but give you clues at least. A system that indicates the progress of work in your area shows up any delays you should do something about. A system that informs you about problems in another area alerts you to decide how to cope with the side-effects in your own area. Routines like these can prevent you from being caught napping by predictable events.

— they give you the information you need for many of the decisions you take. For instance, your methods of recording what has happened in the past, or your communication channels with your people and with other managers. Without them, a lot of your decisions might have to be blind leaps into the dark.

— they provide the machinery to get your decisons implemented. There's no point in a decision if there's no way to put it into practice. If it turns out to be unworkable, it weakens your credibility as a manager. So you've decided to make water run uphill. Fine. Now where's the system to make it happen? Who's going to do it and how? Of course, you occasionally *have* to take a decsion that needs a procedure to implement it — but there isn't one. So you've got to create a procedure. You find you've stepped into not one decison but a whole nest of them.

Systems are needed for good decisions. But a system can't *make* a decision. When you're using your judgement, you're taking into account things that are uncertain and unpredictable. That's something no system can do (not yet anyway. Though there are rumours about fifth-generation computer systems that might yet shock us all!).

There's a general idea that decision-making is what you do when you resolve a definite problem. The idea is that a decision is a distinctive sort of act that you do as a manager: it's obvious to you when you're making it, it has a recognisable result, it's a Big Thing. You can say "I've just made a decision" and feel a sense of relief that it's done. You've got it out of the way.

There's nothing particularly wrong about this idea except that it's true for only a tiny proportion of all the decisions that anyone makes in the course of his work. Anyone. The mass of them are his moment-by-moment judgements about the way he's doing something, with the occasional bigger piece of judgement that sets him off doing something different — what convention calls 'a decision'.

Take a job that many managers would say contains no decisions at all — the job of a copy-typist, say. A lot of her job *is* predictable: she's given a pile of handwritten stuff to type. She's expected to get it done within a certain time. She has rules to follow on layout and margins and so on. She has instructions about the number of carbon copies to do. All of these are the routines that control her work.

But now think of what she has to use her judgement about — the decisions she's bound to make *within* that system. She decides the way she sets up each page within the rules of layout: does it look neat and attractive? She decides whether she's understood the handwriting: should she ask the writer what he meant here and there? She decides how to match her speed of typing to the need for accuracy. She makes mistakes and corrects them — and decides whether a page looks so messy she should retype it. Often she decides in what order to type the stuff in the pile she's given. It's all decision-making. And don't start saying those decisions are meaningless. They're not to the manager who's waiting for the typing to be done. They're not to her either — they are what create her interest and pride in her work.

As a manager you're there to take decisions. So are your people. Their decisions deal with the smaller questions. Yours deal with the bigger ones. If they're only concerned with their own work, you're concerned with the way it's coordinated; if they coordinate their work, you coordinate it with work going on elsewhere. If they think just for the moment, you think ahead; if they think ahead for a week, you think ahead for a month. If they can see only problems, you look for solutions; if they can find solutions, you look for bigger problems to tackle. But there are plenty of managers who don't see this. Like the sales supervisor who takes the easy decisions about sales targets himself, but leaves to the salesman the difficult decisions about how they're to be achieved. That's the same as the husband who reckons he takes the big decisions (like sending his kids to a Public School) and leaves to his wife the little things (like budgeting to be able to pay the fees).

The point is that your bigger decisions give you many more things to consider beyond the immediate result you're after. There are more sweeping effects on other things you're trying to get done. There are longer-term effects to calculate. There are deeper implications for your costs and your people to think of. There are wider side-effects on things that don't directly concern you. To make sense of everything that's involved, you've got to simplify it all *somehow*. And that's where something important can easily slip out of sight.

The real skill in making the big, complicated decision lies in keeping its elementary basics in mind: what's the net result you're trying to produce? That's the ball to keep your eye on. It's essentially quite simple — it's the successful execution that's difficult. There are ball-games like that. The fundamentals can be written on a single sheet of paper. But in the heat of the action it's hard enough to keep one rule in mind at a time, let alone obey all those simple principles at once. The great player has that ability, developed by experience and intensive practice that give him almost automatic performance — especially against weaker contestants who can't put him under pressure. The same is true of the best managers at any level. Practice has perfected their decision-making. They make success seem almost easy.

Many 'practical' managers haven't learned this knack. They get impatient with complications they have to boil down for themselves. If a problem isn't obvious, it isn't a problem. If a thing hasn't happened before, it's not going to happen. They don't want to know about the difficulties people down the line are struggling with. They're constantly getting caught out by events they hadn't foreseen, though they were perfectly predictable. Any problem they've learned to live with disappears from view. Because they're so used to it, they've never bothered to examine it to find out what the problem actually is. Because they don't know what it is, they don't know what it's costing.

Because they don't know what it's costing, they can't see the point of putting even a moderate amount of money, time and effort into solving it. They're the contestants who are perpetually under pressures they've created for themselves.

A managers job is to grasp nettles and seize opportunities. If he doesn't, there's an overwhelming probability no one else will. And that's what his biggest decisions consist of. The deadest duck in management is the guy who doesn't take them. Either he doesn't look for them, or he shuts his eyes to them, or he — ducks them. As a result of his ineptitude, both he and his people are regularly putting a lot of effort into achieving minimal results.

If you're a real manager, your decisions point everyone's efforts in the direction that produces the best pay-off for your organisation. The point of having you around to manage their work is that you minimise the amount of it that's needed to achieve any given output. Or to put it another way, to maximise the useful output that's achieved from any given amount of work by your people: "What's the simplest way we can get the best practical result?"

# Does work need managing?

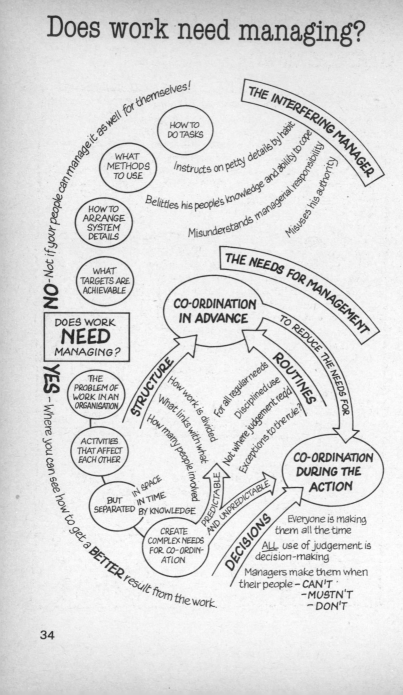

THE INTERFERING MANAGER

HOW TO DO TASKS

WHAT METHODS TO USE

*Instructs on petty details by habit*

HOW TO ARRANGE SYSTEM DETAILS

*Belittles his people's knowledge and ability to cope*

WHAT TARGETS ARE ACHIEVABLE

*Misunderstands managerial responsibility*

*Misuses his authority*

**NO** - Not if your people can manage it as well for themselves!

THE NEEDS FOR MANAGEMENT

CO-ORDINATION IN ADVANCE

TO REDUCE THE NEEDS FOR

DOES WORK **NEED** MANAGING?

STRUCTURE

ROUTINES

THE PROBLEM OF WORK IN AN ORGANISATION

How work is divided
What links with what
How many people involved

For all regular needs
Disciplined use
Not where judgement reqd
Exceptions to the rule?

ACTIVITIES THAT AFFECT EACH OTHER

CO-ORDINATION DURING THE ACTION

BUT SEPARATED

IN SPACE
IN TIME
BY KNOWLEDGE

PREDICTABLE AND UNPREDICTABLE

CREATE COMPLEX NEEDS FOR CO-ORDIN-ATION

DECISIONS

Everyone is making them all the time

ALL use of judgement is decision-making

Managers make them when their people – CAN'T
– MUSTN'T
– DON'T

**YES** – Where you can see how to get a **BETTER** result from the work.

34

# 3. The purpose of the organisation

"Why for heaven's sake are you doing *that*?" is a question that's guaranteed to bring most of us up short. You have to interrupt the train of thought that's chugging along the familiar lines of *what* you're doing and *how*, to ask yourself "well? Why *am* I doing it?" You've got to think a bit to find a suitable reply. Either that, or you sidestep the question with a flip response "just because". You *know* what you're supposed to be doing so why the question? Your attention is on the job in hand — which is actually where it ought to be anyway.

But the *why* question can't be completely ignored in an organisation (treat it how you like in your private life). Someone has to ask it of every piece of the action that goes on. The purpose of doing the things that are done isn't totally self-evident — and it can't be taken for granted by the managers responsible for getting them done. Without some clear and settled idea about the purpose, neither manager — nor worker, for that matter — can know what's *important* to concentrate on in the way the work is done.

In an organisation, the reason for everything that's done ought logically to connect at some point with the purpose of the organisation itself. And it's the management job to see that the connections are made, otherwise time and effort are quite likely to be frittered away on non-essentials while essentials get forgotten. But to do that, you have to see the organisation's purpose in a way that helps to explain the things people are doing inside it. That's where problems often begin.

There's a common idea about business organisations that their real underlying purpose is to make a profit. That isn't in fact a very helpful guide to their managers, because it does very little to explain the things they and their people spend their time doing. In fact more often than not it simply misdirects managers' attention from what they *ought* to be concentrating on. To quote the complaint of the chairman of a Swedish company with subsidiaries in Britain: "our English managers take pride in profit and relationships, but not so much in what we make". It's a fairly common management view in this country that a manufacturing outfit is a contraption for making money upon which the products themselves are a constraint, if not a bloody nuisance. Perhaps that's why so many aren't very good at making profits. It makes more sense to turn the idea around — to see the products themselves as the real purpose, upon which the need for profit acts as the constraint — the 'bloody nuisance'.

Try working it out. Suppose you're talking to a manager in a business organisation who insists that profit is its real purpose.

Ask him whose profit he's talking about and he'll say ''the firm's profit of course'', to which the next question is ''so why does the firm *need* to make a profit?'' If he hasn't started regarding you as someone who's right off his hinges by this time, he might eventually concede that as far as the firm itself is concerned the real point of profit is the firm's survival. No profit, no investors, no company. That doesn't explain *why* the firm needs to survive. Just to make more profit? That's like saying ''I've got to eat to live, so the purpose of living is to eat more and more''.

Of course a business organisation has to earn a profit. But profit isn't its *purpose*. It has to employ people too. But employment isn't its purpose either. Profit governs shareholders' and bankers' willingness to put money into it, sure enough. Employment explains politicians' interest in encouraging industrial growth. But neither shareholders nor politicians do things *inside* an organisation where the work goes on. They influence only the climate in which it lives. This doesn't deny that the economic climate is hugely important in moulding the ways organisations try to achieve their purpose. But it doesn't alter the purpose itself, any more than the weather alters the ultimate purpose of a farm. The weather may make the farmwork easier or more difficult, but it doesn't change the fact that it has got to be done. A purpose has to explain what people in the organisation actually *do* — and should strive to do *better*.

If profit can't explain that, what else can? In many organisations the main purpose seems to be nothing more than to carry on doing the things they always have done. Instead of profit-centred thinking, their managements suffer from production-centred thinking, — which is just as bad if not worse. In some of them, people do take an enormous pride in the end-products of their labours but don't relate those end-products to what's happening in the world outside. In others, managers' and workers' self-satisfaction with their input of effort seems to be the goal. That attitude has been the death of more business organisations and even whole industries than you could shake a stick at. Remember the motor-cycle industry? The ship-building industry? The machine-tool industry? They weren't killed by making poor quality products, but by making the wrong products in the wrong way.

And it still goes on. It's a normal condition of management thinking in many, many business organisations — and even more in public bodies like departments of the civil service and local authorities, in water boards and energy corporations, in schools and hospitals. Their actions are governed primarily by what suits

37

their own convenience. Their managers and staff have become so wrapped up with their organisations' internal workings that they become deaf and blind to what their public thinks. If outsiders such as customers don't happen to like the results, their complaints are dismissed as unreasonable, irrelevant and ignorant.

Yet the one really constructive purpose you can find for all the work that goes on in an organisation lies in what it does for people in the society it serves — its 'customers': it makes articles for them, or provides hotels for them, or holds their money in safe-keeping, or cares for them when they're ill, or educates them as children. In one way or another, whether it's a manufacturer or a hotel company or a bank or a hospital or a school, it serves a 'market'. If it's a business, the purpose that *ought* to explain all the work people do inside it is to **create customers** — to produce a style and quality of end-result that enables it to compete successfully in the market-place. Of how many organisations can you say that that is the kind of purpose their managers and workforces actually strive for?

If the organisation is an arm of public administration, things are different of course. It doesn't need to create customers. They are created for it by politicians and laws. *But it still has a market* — those members of the public who are forced to use its services. They may have no alternative, or perhaps they can't afford the alternatives that exist. If it is an authority of some kind — an income tax office say, or a planning department in a local council — they can't legally avoid using its service! Then the organisation's purpose becomes **to satisfy the public** — to provide the best service it can to local communities or across the nation at the smallest practicable cost to the public purse. The job of an Inspector of Taxes is to ensure everyone pays the state what they're legally obliged to pay: one of his 'customers' is the State (which, after all, is only the total mass of us the public and our public institutions). But beyond that he also has a duty to operate the system in a fair and human way — to see that the individual taxpayer isn't asked to pay more than the law says he should: the taxpayer is his 'customer' too. In both senses, his purpose is 'to satisfy the public'. To be fair, a lot of tax inspectors do try to do the right thing for *both* parts of their composite 'customer'.

If you do think in this way about the purpose of your organisation, your thinking is 'market-centred'. Act as a manager on the basis of that kind of thinking, and you turn your work and that of the people you control into part of your organisation's 'marketing' effort. Marketing in its broad sense is the purpose of *any* kind of managed organisation. It's usually thought of as relevant only to businesses. But as a way of directing what an organisation is trying to do in the society it serves, its reach includes almost every public service too. It consists very simply of seeing the outsiders who benefit from the organisation's work — whether they're customers or the public generally — as the mainspring of *everything* that goes on inside it.

There's a fine source of confusion here in many organisations that think they've got the message. Their response is often to create Marketing Departments and appoint Marketing Managers, which only goes to show how far away they are from understanding the point. Often they're using the term 'marketing' merely to avoid that nasty word 'selling' (as though any business organisation should be ashamed of admitting that it has to sell to its customers). How often do you hear people talk about 'marketing a product' when they mean *selling* it? Sometimes it's used as a name for what is really a market research or sales support activity. Marketing isn't what goes on in one department or job. It is what *every* department and job is at in one way or another. The effect of labelling one bit of the organisation 'marketing' is to tell everyone else that they're not involved. What does that leave as the purpose of their organisation for *them*?

Many supervisors, managers even, will deny any connection between marketing and the work they're managing. If they're in sales, probably not. There's a chance they won't if they're in something like purchasing or despatch. But they're very likely to regard marketing as totally irrelevant if they're in finance or personnel or down among the production workers — or in almost any department of a public service. Is the connection so difficult to see? Purpose there must be in *any* work. The proposition is simple: in an organisation, there's one and only one purpose that adequately explains what *everyone* is doing. Ultimately every job, every task, every decision, every act is done for the customer. And if it isn't? As far as the organisation is concerned, it's wasted.

Marketing is often summed up as 'getting the right product into the right place in the right quantity at the right time and at the right price' — 'right' in each case for the customer of course. That's a very simple way of looking at it, but even that simple definition, if it had been applied to British motor-cycles in the 1960s, might have saved the industry. Instead, at a time when

Italian and Japanese manufacturers had realised that the 'right product' for the market had become small low-powered machines, the foremost British manufacturer was still intent on producing the 'right products' to win TT races. Beautiful big machines, but they fell further and further behind in the race to win *customers.*

But getting the physical end-product right — whether it's motorcycles or medical treatment — isn't all there is to marketing, important as it is. There are a number of other things that have to be got right too. They're all facets of the organisation's work that have an impact on the world outside, that influence its success in 'creating customers' or 'satisfying the public'. All of them centre on the organisation's idea of its 'customer', whoever that is:

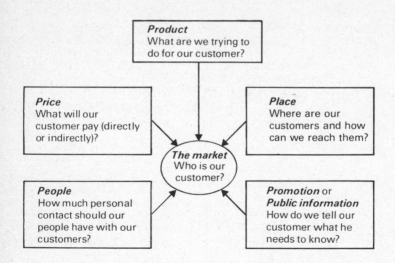

The point is that all of these things affect each other. Change the kind of 'customer' you're trying to serve, and you've got to change everything else to suit. Change the 'product' and that might change the 'promotion' that is best for it and the best policy on its 'price'. Change the amount of personal contact your people have with your market, and that might in practice change the 'product' itself very considerably — as we shall see...

# The Market

*Who is our customer?*

The central question is fundamental. If an organisation can't find a clear way of answering it, its thinking can't be 'market-centred'. A muddled answer doesn't give the thinking anything to centre on.

But usually there isn't an easy, clear answer. Rarely is it single or obvious — perhaps never. Take a manufacturer of — what shall we say? Steak and kidney puddings. Who *is* his customer? The housewife who buys them at the local grocers for her family's evening meal? Her family who actually eat the stuff? ("Wow! can I have more, Mum?") The grocer himself? The wholesaler who supplied the grocer and who bought from the manufacturer in the first place? They all form a kind of composite 'customer', and the manufacturer has to know in his bones what's important about his puddings for every last one of them. It affects the ingredients he buys, the way he processes them, the way he packages the results. It affects the way he advertises them, sells them, distributes them. It affects the price he charges for them. There's nothing in his whole organisation that *isn't* touched in some way by the answer he finds for the question: "Who *is* my customer?"

Or take a newspaper. It has two obvious markets to serve — its readers, and the people and organisations who advertise in its pages. Even that simple fact is complicated enough to cause continual friction between its Editorial and Advertisement departments over who the 'real' customer is. The proper answer is neither one. They *both* go to make up a sort of composite customer. Somehow the two departments have to get into their heads a picture of that composite — a picture that's clear enough for both of them to balance their different customers' interests in the newspapers they create. Usually they fail. They simply go on pulling in different directions whenever there's a conflict of interests.

And if you think that's quite enough to be going on with, hold on! Ask the lads in the Circulation Department who the customer is — "our newsagents of course". Ask the girls who sell space in the classified ads columns over the phone, and (if it's a local newspaper) they'll talk about local people and small businesses who want something or who've got the odd item to sell. Ask the boys who sell the big display ads and they'll talk about big companies. Ask the folk writing news items, or those on the sports desk, or those retailing local gossip — they'll all give you different answers. Do you see how complex that composite is getting? Somehow, every paper *does* find an answer. But whether it's an answer that gives everyone who works in the place a clear sense — and the *same* sense — of their newspaper's purpose is usually quite a different matter.

And the same goes for any organisation you can think of. Hotels that have to balance the differing requirements of residents and local night-outers. Schools that can't decide whether they're there to serve the interests of the kids or their parents or the local employers or the education committee — or of their own teaching staff's political inclinations, for that matter. The roads and transport departments of local authorities who are pulled one way by Big Business with its huge lorries, another way by the local residents who have somehow to live in the place. If an organisation doesn't find a good balance, it's simply pushed hither and thither by each wave of pressure that surges at it. If it does find a balance, then it has a stable centre for its thinking about the way it is trying to satisfy its market.

Sometimes the problem is one of getting the centre wrong — of failing to see the way a market is changing. That was the real problem for the motor-cycle industry. It was also the hole that Smiths Potato Crisps fell into in the 1960s. They had found the obvious single answer to the question for their products: people in pubs ate crisps. Their packaging, their selling methods, their distribution, their pricing was all geared to that simple proposition. It wasn't until Golden Wonder had shown the way and had driven Smiths near the point of no return that they woke up to the enormous new market that existed in the supermarkets opening up throughout the country. The customer was eating crisps at home!

For any organisation — the one you work in for instance — the point of all this is that it *ought* to influence almost anything anyone does in the outfit. If you don't know which customers you're trying to serve how can you decide what to provide them with? How can you decide how to approach them, what information to give, how your people should treat them? How can you decide what is an acceptable cost for what the organisation does for them? And these questions have a bearing on everything else that's done *inside* the organisation — how it's structured, the resources it needs, the systems it uses, the jobs its people do, the way they're managed... Everything ought to relate back to that prime question: who is our customer?

If there's anything that distinguishes the really successful organisations in any field from their weaker brethren, it's this: they have a very clear idea of the market they've chosen to serve; it's market that they can and do serve superbly well; and it's a market in which they can live and be healthy — meaning financially healthy. Maybe an absolutely crystal-clear picture of the 'customer' isn't ever possible, but they've got a heap closer to it than their profit-centred or production-centred rivals. And it's not a picture that's locked away in the minds of the Board or the 'Marketing Managers'. *Everyone* shares it. The Chairman, the managers and supervisors, the salesmen out in the field, the lads on the production floor, the girls on the switchboard, the clerks in the accounts office. It's what gives all of them pride in the organisation they work for.

In case you work in the area of public service and think this doesn't apply to your organisation, why shouldn't it? There *are* some differences of course. The organisation isn't free to choose its market — as we've said, that is chosen for it by politicians and laws. And just how healthy an existence the organisation can live depends *partly* on the amount of public money they make available to it. Partly, not totally, because every organisation has some freedom to cut its coat according to its cloth. The trouble has been — in the past at any rate — that a lot of public organisations have been cutting to the full width of the cloth regardless of the size of the coat that's needed. When the cloth is made narrower in an attempt to force really economic working on the fat parts of public bodies, they often contrive to continue their wasteful methods of cloth-cutting.

They simply reduce the quality of the coat — the standards of the service they give their market, the public.

But however politicians try to define your market and the service it's to be offered, it's too complex a picture for them to rule every line and dot. There's still a need for officers and their staff to refine it further, to find the best balances between the different public interests involved — and to look for more efficient methods of cloth-cutting! Standards of service *don't* depend totally on the resources available. They also depend on the sense of purpose and skill with which the resources are used. (Did you know that in a restaurant you can actually get *worse* service if there are too many waiters on duty?) A very simple instance: it doesn't actually cost any more for officers and staff to be courteous to the members of the public they meet, but it does a hell of a lot for the public's idea of the quality of the service — the 'product' they're getting. Why do so many people in public service not seem to care if they come over to the public as officious, patronising and overbearing? Is it because they don't feel the public are really their *customers*?

Like the successful business enterprise, the arm of public administration that's really doing an effective job has a clear idea of its market — which means a fair and consistent way of balancing the interests of the various parts of the 'public' it is trying to serve. It serves that market to the best standards it is capable of achieving. And it keeps itself lean, energetic and economic enough to achieve that goal within the limits of the available resources. There are no excess bodies or activities wasted in places they're *not* needed, while the places they *are* needed to serve the market are starved...

Once it's clear *who* the customer is, the organisation then has to work out what that implies for each of those five facets of its marketing.

# 1. 'Product'

*What are we trying to do for our customer?*

The question isn't quite as straight forward as you might suppose. There are two ways of taking it — one obvious, the other not-so-obvious.

The obvious meaning is the sort of answer each organisation finds for this question:

## What kind of 'product' does our customer need?

The question asks the organisation to look at the end-results of its work, whatever they are — goods or services — from the point of view of the customer. Do they have the kind of features that make them right for the market they're intended for?

Car owners don't all look for the same sort of car. Each model has to be designed for its own part of the total market for cars. Once its market has been decided, then it's a matter of working out exactly what sort of car those customers will be attracted by — its appearance, performance, comfort, capacity, reliability, running costs, safety... The list is a long one. All its items have to be put together to make a package of qualities that best appeals to the intended customers.

Or take a hotel: what is *its* 'product'? Don't say simply 'satisfied guests', because the question is *which* guests and *what* kinds of satisfaction. That raises all sorts of issues to do with the service the hotel ought to offer: the kind of welcome those guests expect, the standards of accommodation they'll look for, the sorts of menu they'll find attractive, the manner of the staff towards them, the general atmosphere of the place. Part of the 'product' is even the building itself — old oak beams, or smart modernity. Everything in it goes to make the hotel more appealing to some people who use hotels, less so to others. Having decided which are its own best market, the hotel can then try to create the kind of service that best satisfies those particular customers.

In fact, the more you think about the end-results of your organisation's work from the market viewpoint, the more angles you'll find that are all part of the 'product'. But when they're all added up, they amount to a need to match that total product to its market in three main ways:

- in its *design*
- in its *craftsmanship*
- in its *availability*

Try it in practice. Take two very different 'products' — an appliance of some kind (a pocket calculator say, or a kitchen stove) and the education provided by a school:

**Design:** in the case of the appliance this is the total package of things like:

- its functions and shape
- its basic engineering
- the technology it incorporates

- its appearance and finish
- its intended life and reliability
- its ease of maintenance
- the after-sales servicing it will need

In the case of the school, the design of its education lies in the way it blends together such things as:

- what the school sets out to achieve (exam results? The development of practical abilities? The attitudes and values absorbed by the children?).
- the subjects taught in its syllabus.
- teaching methods and technology.
- how its classes are organised (sizes, grades etc.).
- its accommodation and how it's used.
- rules of conduct and the strength of discipline.
- career-guidance and the school's relationship with local employers.

**Craftsmanship:** for the appliance this means what's put into its manufacture by the workforce:

- the kinds of skill they apply.
- the quality of the work they do.
- the efficiency with which faulty items are rejected.
- the motivation of the workforce (their pride in the product?).

For the school it's a matter of the standards of the teaching — and that depends on the teaching staff:

- their understanding of the children's needs.
- their ability to handle the classes they teach.
- their knowledge and skill as teachers.
- the general state of their morale.

**Availability:** for the appliance, this asks whether the thing is produced in the volume needed *when* it's needed:

- can the firm offer the delivery its customers require?
- is there a seasonal pattern in the demand? Does the firm cope with it successfully?
- is the firm selling within the limits of its resources to supply? Or are over-optimistic production schedules causing scamped work in the factory and broken delivery promises to customers?
- is management using the resources properly? Or is bad organisation and poor scheduling of work wasting some of the capacity that's actually there, causing unacceptable delays in deliveries to customers?

For the school, it's a question of its capacity to provide the intended standard of education for the children it has to accommodate:

- what is the size of its 'market' — the number of children who want places in it?
- how many children can the school accept before the design of its education can't cope, and the craftsmanship of its teaching begins to suffer?
- if its capacity is overstretched, can it redesign its educational goals and methods to satisfy its market in a different way? How can the morale and spirit of its staff be maintained? Or must it accept as inevitable a lower standard in the craftsmanship of its teaching?

What's more, these things don't stand still. If *your* organisation doesn't develop an improvement in the design of its product or its craftsmanship or its availability, be sure another one will soon. Do you know the story of the stainless steel razor-blade? It's history now, but it illustrates a point that's as true today as it was then. Before that product was launched into the market-place, Gillette held some 80% of the U.K. razor-blade market. But it wasn't Gillette who burst in with stainless steel — it was Wilkinson Sword. By the time the fracas was over, Gillette's market share had dropped to a mere 30% or so. It has re-captured most of that lost market now of course, but *it didn't need to lose it in the first place*.

For many, many organisations — private business or public service — the main barrier to their achievement of their marketing purpose (and what other purpose have they got?) is the dismal quality of the product they're offering. Often it's because its design is either wrong for the market they're in, or wrong for any conceivable market they *could* be in. It's just thoroughly bad. Products that are aimed at the cheap end of the market (which is where a lot of public service must aim its products) don't *have* to be poorly designed. A lot of them are, but that doesn't necessarily save the organisation any money, and they do its reputation harm. At other times it's the product's craftsmanship that's the problem, bespeaking a shocking mis-management — or *non*-management — of the people and processes that produce it.

But as often, the problem is that what's being attempted is itself ridiculous. Which leads to the other, not-so-obvious meaning in the 'product' question for each organisation to answer:

> *Is our total 'product' designed in such a way that we can actually provide it?*

A product may be badly designed, not for its market, but for the craftsmanship it demands from the workforce: they may not possess the skills needed to do it that way, or they may be unmotivated to supply the effort that's required. On the other hand, if the craftsmanship *is* available, it may open up a wider range of choice about the way the thing is designed. Or again, the design may be fine for the customers — but impossible to supply in the volume required within the available resources. Another design that satisfies the customers equally well may avoid those problems of over-stretched capacity.

What gives our industry its worst name is its inability to manage the availability of its products — their delivery. A few years ago, a report appeared on an investigation of nearly two-hundred factories in this country, mostly in engineering. Its findings were devastating:

- only 3% delivered all their orders on time
- 80% delivered more than one in every ten orders late.
- 25% delivered more than *five* in every ten orders late.
- 3% delivered every single order late.

What on earth was the standard of delivery performance they aimed to achieve? No more than one-in-ten orders late is hardly very ambitious, and it's depressing if an organisation thinks it's

48

doing well if it does no better than that. Yet the problem wasn't shortage of time. Most of the deliveries in this case were promised in two months or more. For one the promise was two years.

The real problem lay in what the firms were trying to do. Many were making a hotch-potch of standard goods mixed in the made-to-order goods. Often the range of their end-products was too wide for their resources and their management abilities to cope with: it was typical for new products to be added to the range without old products being taken out of it. And some companies complicated things still further by failing to decide whether they were in the business of making cheap, off-the-peg, mass-produced items or higher-priced, hand-tailored, customer-choice stuff. They tried to do *both* at the same time. It wasn't just that they designed their 'product' — the total thing they were attempting in the market-place — badly. They hadn't *designed* it at all!

In the work that goes on in an organisation, it's usually the product itself that creates the biggest pile of management decisions — and if they're *not* taken or are taken all wrong, of management headaches too. The headaches often get passed on to the customer. Who can blame him if he complains — or simply looks elsewhere for what he needs?


## 2. 'Place'

*Where are our customers?*

The second facet of marketing takes account of the problems of reaching the intended customers and the way the product arrives. The product is here. The customer is there. How does it get to him — or how does he get to it? Whichever way around, one or the other has to happen.

For physical products, whether they're cars, cookers or packets of crisps, this is a question of their **distribution**: the shops or other outlets they're put into and the transport arrangements that get them there. In fact, for many products there's quite a chain of places they have to pass through before they reach the place where the actual customer first glimpses them: from the organisation's finished goods store to its depots up and down the country, from there to distributors' warehouses and on to retailers' own storerooms — and eventually to the shelves in the shop. That's not the only alternative of course. A system of delivery direct to the customer may sometimes make more sense for the product, its market, and even for the organisation itself.

But however distribution is done, it creates another heap of management decisions — and if they're wrong, a further heap of management problems:

- where can the product best find the customers it's designed for? In what sorts of areas and outlets?
- how efficient and reliable is the distribution system to those outlets? (There's no point in having the capacity to make the thing if what's made doesn't reach the shops in the right volume and at the right time for the demand).
- how flexible is the system to respond to variations in the demand? Can it handle peaks and troughs in a seasonal market? Can it cope with special orders, sudden shortages — or even the weather?
- in what condition will the product arrive? Is it designed to stand up to the kinds of handling and storage it will get? What kind of packaging does it need to protect it? What are the risks of 'shrinkage' as it's delicately called — i.e. thieving?
- what's its 'shelf-life'? (That might be a crucial question if it's something like bread or newspapers. Both get stale if they don't move through the system fast enough!)
- how well can the system respond to requests or complaints from the market? Where will the retailer be expected to cope? How should the firm organise itself to deal with those he can't (or won't) handle?
- how efficient is the administrative system by which distribution is controlled? Is the information flow fast and reliable? Is it easy to find out quickly the situation on every order in the system?
- what's the strength of the competition at the outlets chosen? Is the product itself attractive enough to meet that competition for the customers there?

Products can't be designed *only* for the needs of the market and the capabilities of the production department. As often as not, their design also has to allow for the system that distributes them. The shape of a food product and its packaging has to fit into warehouse storage at one point and on to supermarket shelves at another. A table may be designed to go through the system in dismantled form but to be easy for the customer to re-assemble. The date printed on each issue of an international weekly magazine has to allow for the time-lag in foreign postal systems before it reaches its subscribers out there. But the same applies in reverse too: the system has to be chosen to suit the product. If you're selling eggs, you don't send them through the post!

But what about the 'product' that's actually a service? If you think about it, the 'place' question for an organisation like a shop or hotel or bank or hospital is actually one of its own **location**. *It's market is restricted by the place it's in.* Not entirely perhaps — a big London department store may draw its customers from far afield; a specialist hospital may have the whole country as its market. But apart from extreme examples like these, a lot of service organisations are limited by their geography. A bank in a small country town may have to accept that the local farming community is one of its best markets. So its 'product' — the bank services it concentrates on and the way it organises itself to provide them — has to be designed to suit a market that's determined by its own location. The market of potential guests for a hotel is created as much by its site as by the kind of service it aims to provide. If it's a city centre hotel, it can hardly set its sights at the huntin', shootin' and fishin' fraternity! That still leaves plenty of scope among the markets that do exist in its locality. Does it aim its 'product' of services and atmosphere at the visiting businessman? The conference

51

trade? The tourist market? And which part of the local population does it try to attract into its bars and restaurant? What are the problems if its markets don't mix — if the different types of guests don't go particularly well together, if the things they want are mutually impossible to provide?

All of these questions of distribution or location have implications for the management of the organisation. The tentacles of their effects reach deep into its inner workings, creating a pressure point here, a need for improved planning or extra resources there. And they have an over-riding influence over the next of the facets of marketing — the way a business promotes its product, the way a public body informs its public.

## 3. 'Promotion' or 'Public information'

*How do we tell our customer what he needs to know?*

Whenever 'marketing' is mentioned in a commercial organisation, this third facet is what everyone seems to think about: how is the product PROMOTED? But now that you're getting to grips with what market-centred thinking in an organisation actually means, you'll see it takes its place as one angle on it. It's *not* the whole story. There's no future in complaining about the sales force's dismal results if the real problem is in the product's design, or if it has earned a deservedly poor reputation in the market-place for its quality or delivery, or if it can't be produced at a reasonable cost because of inefficient and uneconomic methods of working. To tackle a problem that shows up out in the sales field, you have to find out where it starts — and that may be deep inside the organisation itself.

Which is not to deny that the selling itself is frequently the weak link. But when it is, it may not be altogether the fault of the salespeople themselves. It has often got more to do with the way that the total promotional effort is organised. In most organisations, there are three main elements in their approach to their markets that have to work in harmony:

- the *advertising* that's done on television, in newspapers, by direct mail letters...
- how the *salesforce* is structured and managed.
- the way the product's own *packaging* is designed to appeal.

Remember that the decisions made on all these elements have to be taken with an eye to the things we've dealt with already *Who* are the customers? *What* is the 'product' being offered to them? *Where* is it being placed in the market?

**ADVERTISING** is something that every business organisation has to do in one way or another. You may think that's obvious, but there are plenty of firms that didn't see it and have reaped the results of their failure. Remember 'Vim'? Once upon a time it was the market leader among scouring powders. Its management reckoned they didn't need to spend good money on advertising — *everyone* knew 'Vim'. Within a few years it was struggling to keep a toe-hold in the market-place.

But there's advertising and advertising. Not all products need the full panoply of press and TV campaigns. Many do better with the derided sales letter popped through letter-boxes around the country (Don't sneer: Readers Digest does very well with its direct mail shots. If *you* don't read them, *someone* obviously does.) A small organisation might survive quite happily on a reputation for quality and service that's passed around by satisfied customers plus a regular small ad in the local paper. And there are many more possibilities, from huge outdoor bill-boards to small brochures.

The methods of advertising are legion, but so are its purposes in the promotional strategies of different organisations. If an outfit is selling its product through other people's retail shops, for instance, it's own salesman aren't

53

selling to the *eventual* customer. They're visiting the retailers who are themselves also customers of course. The retailers won't be persuaded to take more of the product unless they can see the customer — *their* customer — is buying it. How does the organisation reach its eventual customer? By advertising, of course. The purpose of its advertising is to 'pull its product through the retail outlets', as they say.

In one way or another, a lot of advertising is aimed at getting the customer to *do* something: to pick a product off a supermarket shelf, or to go somewhere where a service is available — to a department store or a hotel or a bank. Or it may start something that will eventually wind up with a sale — to get him to lift a telephone or fill in an enquiry form. But that's not always the aim. Sometimes it is to get him into the right frame of mind for a later direct approach by a salesman. More often than you might expect, it is simply to make him feel favourably inclined towards the organisation itself ('prestige advertising' as it is called).

Occasionally advertisements have a double-edged purpose. A few years ago a crop of them appeared on bill-boards throughout the London underground: 'Top People take The Times'. Their obvious purpose was to appeal to the 'top people' who weren't readers of the newspaper. Their underlying purpose (and probably the real one) was to attract the potential advertiser: if he wanted to reach the decision-makers in the organisations that were *his* market, those people, as 'top people', would of course be reading The Times.

Often enough, an organisation's advertising has to be geared to changes in its market-place (to meet some vigorous competition, say) or to developments in its product of its product's availability. It has to respond to the limitations imposed by distribution channels or by the location of the organisation itself. And it has to be planned to help the salesforce in *their* efforts to sell.

**THE SALES FORCE** is the main force in most companies' selling. Ultimately the whole of almost every business organisation depends on its salesmen's skill and commitment. Surprisingly enough, that's not the first question for its management. There's something even more fundamental: whatever the sales force is trying to do, does that purpose make sense in terms of its market and its product? Which raises further questions — about the sort of people the company employs as salesmen, about the way they're organised, about the selling methods they use... If the basics aren't right, there's little point in trying to motivate the salesman to do something that's fundamentally stupid.

Our first book, *What is a Manager?*, mentioned the case of a national organisation that owned a lot of local newspapers — dailies and weeklies published in towns and cities from the north of Scotland to the southern parts of England. Each newspaper had an advertisement sales department with a sales force selling its own paper's advertisement space to local advertisers. The London headquarters of the group also had an advertisement sales force. But their job was to sell space in *all* the group's newspapers to big national advertisers. The group's 'product' for these advertisers was of course the total range of their markets they could reach through the *combined* coverage of the individual newspapers.

Given that 'product' and the need to organise the London salesforce into teams, how would you have arranged the teams? Perhaps by the different industries of the advertisers? This team for the motor industry, say, that one for domestic appliance manufacturers... Perhaps by the types of advertising campaigns the advertisers want to organise? This team for retail support advertising; that one for 'prestige' advertising... Or even perhaps by the advertising agencies the national advertisers use... There are quite a few options.

The one thing you *don't* do is to make each team sell space in the newspapers for one locality: this team selling for the newspapers in Scotland, that team for the north of England... That defeats the whole point of having a *national* spread of local papers to offer to the national advertiser. But that is precisely the way the teams were arranged. Presumably the idea was to make it easy to charge each team's costs back to the publishing centres it was selling for. That seemed to be more important to the overlord of this cockup than the sales results it produced — which were decidedly poor. The whole set-up was a farce, though it's doubtful whether the salesmen themselves saw the joke. Knowing the frustrations it was causing within their teams, the team leaders constantly sought to get it changed. But all to no avail. 'Management' simply couldn't see the point — the need to understand what the 'product' is from the customer's point of view and to organise the sales force to suit.

In decisions about the salesforce, you ignore at your peril the way the customer thinks — meaning the guy who actually makes the decisions whether or not to buy the product from you. Get it wrong and you're likely not only to organise the sales force all wrong. You're also likely to hire the wrong people into it to sell your product to your customer. They'll waste time talking to the person who makes them feel comfortable rather than the one who has the buying authority. And even if by accident they get in front of the right person, they'll try to sell the thing at the wrong time in the wrong way. Technical salesmen are needed if the customers generally are technical people; salesmen with commercial nous are needed if the customers are business people or professional buyers; salesmen with an attractive personality and a persuasive manner may be just the ticket if the market is neither particularly technical nor commercially-minded — and tends to remove the 'welcome' mat from the door when the salesman makes his appearance. There ain't no such animal as the salesman who's equally good in every kind of market. It sounds obvious, but sometimes organisations pick the most unlikely people for the particular selling jobs they want done.

Remember the prime purpose of the organisation: *to create customers*. The sales force is right up at its sharp end to achieve that result. But it cannot succeed if it sees its task as pushing the product on unwilling buyers who don't actually need the thing and can't really afford it, but who give in to a determined con-man's persistence — and regret their decision afterwards. The hard sell *is* a characteristic of some organisations. If they're not fly-by-night, they're fly-within-a-few-years unless they mend their ways. The net result in the long term is a growing resistance to their sales approaches and a determination among those who've been had never to be had again. That's not creating customers. That's just 'making a sale'.

Customers are people who've bought before, and who'll buy again and again. If the organisation is producing the right sort of product to create them, it deserves a sales force that does precisely that: one that creates them and *keeps* them as customers. It's true that many customers need to be persuaded by a skilful salesman. People often *don't* realise what they need, often don't focus their wants clearly enough to know how to satisfy them. The task is to help the customer work out what his wants and needs actually are, and to help him to see how the product satisfies them.

If the fundamental purpose and organisation of the salesforce is right, then you have questions of how it's managed:

> — the allocation of 'territories'. The patch each salesman is to cover, the customers whose business he has to cultivate, the potential customers he should approach.

- the planning of journeys and visits. It has to be planned by *someone* — either the salesman or his boss — to ensure that the time he spends with each customer bears some resemblance to the value of the business he might conceivably get there in the future.
- sales targets. Which ought to be based on a realistic appreciation of what it's actually possible to achieve with the right sort of effort.
- the system of reporting. Not simply to keep tabs on what the sales force are doing. Equally important is the feed-back of their intimate knowledge of what's happening in the market-place. It's one of the basic ingredients to go into the stew-pot that's simmering ideas of product development and other things to do with the organisation's future.

Incidentally, there's a difference between selling and *sales servicing*. A lot of salesmen are employed to do jobs that many a delivery van driver could do — simply seeing the retailer has adequate stocks and arranging to top them up. And don't go and call the van driver a 'van salesman' either. That is, not unless you've found that rare individual who can be delivering a consignment one moment and hey presto! He's a salesman the next. For all that, sales servicing *is* an important part of the sales operation, and a lot of firms that don't have their own delivery fleets (and even some that do) manage it very well. For a product that needs constant replenishment in retail outlets there's a simple solution: a small team of sales service staff phoning retailers on a regular schedule.

The telephone selling idea is one that will spread in this country. Why send a salesman driving around the place and seeing perhaps ten or twenty customers a day, when that same salesman could make a perfectly effective interim contact with perhaps fifty customers in that same day without moving from his desk?

A word of caution. If you're a sales manager or supervisor with an eye to the costs of selling, by all means get your sales team to use the economy of telephone selling. But don't think it's the complete answer. It's only an *interim* contact between the salesman's actual visits out there. There's nothing that can replace the need for your organisation to get him sitting down with the customer, eyeball to eyeball.

**PACKAGING** is the product 'selling itself'. It's also the aspect of promotion that comes closest to the product — quite literally. For a physical product, its original purpose was to protect whatever had been put into the thing's design and craftsmanship as it ran the gauntlet of its channels of distribution into the customer's hands. In that sense it's a part of the product itself, needing design and craftsmanship no less than the thing inside. But soon after it had been invented in the year dot, manufacturers realised it also had potential for a secondary purpose.

With the enormous development in this century of packaging technology and promotional art, the secondary purpose has become the primary one. The main point of the packaging is to attract the customer's eye to the product as he passes by where it sits in the shop window or on the supermarket shelf. It can appeal by arousing his curiosity, by creating an expectation in his mind, even by going along with his subconscious feelings about 'how things should be'. Often its aim is to establish an identity for a product that is otherwise not so very different from a lot of others: he recognises it as an old friend. Most modern packaging goes way beyond the limits of what's needed to protect the product. Wrapper within box within carton within cellophane — its aim is almost to recapture of the customer the fun of 'opening Christmas presents'!

There's a Japanese company making a very impressive malt whisky (apologies to our Scots readers). If the whisky is impressive, its package — the bottle that encases it — is quite fantastic. It is sheathed in a beautifully designed and immensely intricate model of a samurai warrior. The bottle with its sheathing costs about double what the whisky costs to produce. Is the whisky the product and the bottle the package? Or is the bottle the *real* product, and the whisky an excuse for buying it? 'Packaging' and 'product' seem to have reversed their roles in a manner of speaking.

Don't think of packaging in a promotional sense only as the stuff that encases the things you buy in shops. It is, in a broader sense, whatever gains the customer's immediate approval as he first approaches the physical presence of the thing your organisation has to offer. For a shop, its packaging is the shop window and the shopper's first glimpse of the arrangement of the goods inside. For a hotel, it is its frontage and the appearance of its reception area. For an airline it's the way its planes are painted and the uniform of the cabin staff. For an office, it's often its switchboard operator's first words to the incoming call. Even the salesmen and other staff who meet the public have their packaging — their clothes, their appearance and the manner of the welcome they give. They all go to create that vital First Impression that a 'product' gives its customers. Is it the right impression?

Promotion is all about the way a business constructs its contacts with its market. It's to do with the organisation's efforts to see that its customers are informed in a *favourable* way about the 'product', and about the organisation itself. Informed also in a way that's *appropriate* to the different customers' actual needs and interests. Unless the organisation is morally deformed or doing a desperate cover-up job on a poor product ( and whose fault is that?), it's open and honest. If the product is a good one, there's no point in *not* being honest about it. Anyway, concealing things the market ought to know has a nasty tendency of rebounding later. Once word gets out — which it usually does sooner or later — the outfit gets an unpleasant reputation that is difficult to dispel. It loses credibility.

Now if you work in a public service and feel that nothing that has been said about promotion so far has the slightest relevance to *your* organisation, read that last paragraph again. Slowly! If you like, replace the word 'business' by 'public organisation'. The practical details may be different, but the principles are the same. A public body that truly operates in a market-centred way organises and manages its contacts with its market quite as thoroughly as a business does. True, those contacts aren't quite as essential to its continued survival. But they *are* essential to its purpose: 'to satisfy the public'.

'Promotion' for a public organisation means **public information**. Most organs of public service are appallingly bad at it, usually because they haven't got the starting-point right. They don't see the public they serve as the customer. So they don't bother to tell the public anything they haven't *got* to — unless it's something they want to be congratulated about (as if they weren't indulging in enough self-congratulation anyway). If it's something they know the public would be *very* interested to hear (the scandalously bad care provided by an old folks' home, say, or a bit of thoroughly self-interested decision-making in a committee chamber or departmental office), they usually have the almighty impertinence to claim that it's 'not in the public interest' to provide that sort of information. That's if they can't plead the Official Secrets Act or some piece of beaurocratic nonsense that's designed to protect the beaurocrats from the public fury they often deserve.

But in our society it's impossible to keep *everything* hidden.

Corners of the rug are occasionally lifted by the reporters of national or local newspapers to reveal the appalling dereliction and mismanagement (or very often, *non*-management) that's underneath. Now and again a whole piece of rug is whipped away by true public servants like Leslie Chapman. Have you heard of him? He has written two books that have done a remarkable job of rug-removing. Each tells a factual story that is a public disgrace, and that the public officials concerned had been at great pains to keep out of the public eye — *real* 'public information'. One was produced shortly after he resigned from a job as a regional director of a large department in the civil service: *Your Disobedient Servant*. The other chronicles his attempts since then to introduce effective management into the London Transport Executive (he failed) and two local authorities (one a total failure, the other only a partial success). For once, the blurb on a book cover — the one on his second book, *Waste Away* — said nothing more than the truth: ''Mr. Chapman has performed an inestimable public service''.

The sad truth is that not only do officers and staff in public service conceal the facts of their failures from the public. They themselves prefer not to look at the facts. It's not just a question of recognising and accepting that the public is getting a rotten deal. That's not enough. You then have to find out what's going wrong to *cause* that rotten deal — the 'product' that the public is, not offered, but forced to accept: in most cases there's no practicable alternative. That means looking at every aspect of the work that's actually done inside each organisation, and trying to manage it properly to achieve a coherent purpose. What other can there be than 'to satisfy the public'? Any attempts to get the public information part of its marketing right can't work unless all the *other* parts are reasonably near right as well — the product, the place, the people *and* the price (which was Leslie Chapman's prime criticism, the lack of genuine effort in public bodies to stop wasting the public's money).

When all of those things are right, a public organisation might conceivably apply some of its management thinking to the way it keeps its market properly informed:

> — informed about what its 'product' actually provides, with no intention of letting the public think the product is better than it actually is. Why *shouldn't* parents know the exam results a school is achieving?
>
> — informed about what is going on and why. For instance, if roadworks are going to change traffic routes temporarily, treating the information to local residents

and others who'll be affected as part of the design of the whole project rather than something inconsequentially tacked on at the end.

— informed about the organisation itself — how it is working to provide its product at the right price. If the customer doesn't have the opportunity to refuse the deal, he at least has a right to some evidence that the cost to him in taxes and rates or whatever is the outcome of a reasonable sense of economy within the organisation.

Its methods of doing this also need to be looked at for their coherence in a properly-organised system:

**ADVERTISING** has an obvious role: information to the public generally about services provided, legal notices and statutory requirements, projects being considered and their implications... Just as in business advertising, this isn't only a question of newspaper ads. Forms, leaflets, booklets, circular letters, even the time-tables that are (or aren't) provided at bus-stops all count in one way or another. Now and again it's worth taking a look at how efficiently they're all being used in combination to tell the public what it needs to know about the organisation and its product, or to enable the customer to 'order the product' (i.e. fill in a form).

But besides what they're actually saying, they convey an impression of the attitude of the organisation towards its public too. Officials have a dreadful habit of writing to their public in a pompous, longwinded and obscure kind of English. They sound too conscious of themselves as representing 'authority' rather than 'service'. The attitude that comes through is one of beaurocratic self-importance and total disregard of the need to make things clearly understandable. There's no attempt to show the organisation as one that's concerned about being helpful. If the public doesn't understand, it's the public's fault!

A small set-up called 'The Plain English Campaign' has been battling against this tide of sludge with some effect. Run by two energetic and remarkably public-spirited people, Martin Cutts and Chrissie Mather, it has succeeded in persuading both public bodies and business organisations to write their letters, forms and notices in a more simple, direct and friendly style. The range of targets has included government departments, local authorities, public corporations, insurance companies — even the Chief Parliamentary Legal Draughtsman. But should their efforts have become necessary in the first place?

**PRESS INFORMATION** is a huge source of public information, often of stuff that this or that arm of public administration would have preferred not to be revealed. But it has a positive function too, and one that is not generally available to the vast mass of business. *The press is interested in what politicians and public officials are doing.* Rightly used, that interest creates a broad channel of information that is available to be integrated with all the stuff that goes down the advertising route. And it's a channel that doesn't cost the organisation a bean, apart from the willingness to spend a bit of time, talking to the reporter. There's economy for you!

The snag is that usually the senior officials insist that their juniors don't talk to the press. That's probably understandable if the seniors are afraid of the juniors letting some unfortunate cat out of the bag, or doubt their loyalty or ability to put the right gloss on a story. But in that case, there's something wrong with their management. If the organisation is being run right and the product is good, there oughtn't to be that many unfortunate cats around the place. And if the juniors understand what their organisation is trying to do and are proud of it, they should be able to speak with as much loyalty and common-sense about it as anyone else. It's an organisation that is badly managed and has things to hide that needs rules about the Press only speaking to its top people.

**THE TELEPHONE** has its part to play. Heaven knows, even businesses can be very lackadaisical about the impression the customer receives when his call reaches the telephone receptionist. Public service is infinitely worse. Try phoning *your* office to listen to the manner in which your call is answered — and remember, what you're hearing is part of your organisation's 'packaging' as far as your market is concerned. Is the voice clear, bright, welcoming? For all the person who picks up the phone knows, you're a customer.

**MEETING THE PUBLIC** is often a major part of the job of many a public official — perhaps not so surprisingly. This is the 'people' facet of marketing which we're going to deal with next. Here we're thinking of how the organisation talks about something to do with the 'product' to the people who represent its 'market'. In other words, the public service equivalent of the function of a sales force in a business.

If your organisation's staff go out to the public, is there some kind of system about the way they do it? Things like territory allocations and journey planning don't apply only to salesmen. The point of the first is to enable each of your staff to become familiar with his patch — to get to know the people who are affected by your outfit's work in one area of its operation, to form good working relationships with them, to understand their real needs and their feelings about the service they get. The point of the second is to use his time efficiently. And whether your people visit the public or the public visits them, there should be some systematic reporting-back on what has happened, what they've found out. That's a key element in the management of any group of people who meet their organisation's customers.

## 4. 'People'

*How much personal contact should our people have with our customers?*

The fourth facet of marketing is a question of how many people in the organisation actually meet the people out there in its market as a normal, regular part of their job. Often it's the most difficult part of marketing to manage successfully.

The skill of constantly meeting people you don't know and of being able to cope in an easy, positive way with the human pressures involved isn't all that common. That is to say, a lot of people can't do it very well, or *don't* do it very well — the difference is immaterial to a customer. Sure, they're fine talking to people they know, even better with people they like. But meeting someone they haven't met before, they aren't at ease; they don't know what to say that will put the *other* person at ease; they find it difficult to initiate a conversation on something they want to talk about without being abrupt; they can't handle a point of disagreement pleasantly but firmly.

It may sound a small thing but it's important: do you notice how many people don't *smile* whenever they meet a customer in the context of work? Shop assistants, the girls at supermarket checkouts, counter clerks in the post office, the man who pops in to read the gas meter, the delivery van driver. Facing one of their organisation's customers, many people's normal expression is either an earnest and faintly harassed look, or one of being preoccupied with something else.

If you happen to make a teasing comment about it (with a smile on *your* face of course), the response is quite likely to be a snappy "you can't have everything, you know", as though you're asking a favour for yourself. It's *their* organisation the favour would be done for — a tiny favour for you, to earn a bigger favour for the organisation *from* you, in the shape of your continued goodwill and custom. But no, they need time to warm to the other person, and in dealing with a string of customer contacts, time is what you haven't got. A smile has got to be an instant reaction to each new face, or forget it.

With many kinds of commercial enterprise whose product is *goods,* a solid tangible something, the only people who actually need to meet the customer are the members of the sales force. That's their job. And a tough, demanding job it is for the salesman who's trying to do it right. It's one of the toughest spots to be in the whole organisation.

Just think of the situation he's in day in, day out. He *is* the organisation for the people he meets. He has to cope successfully with all those human pressures that the job involves, continually sticking his neck into situations where he can't be sure what sort of reception he'll get. He takes the stick from the people who matter — the customers — for the failings of every other member of the whole outfit. A daft idea the chairman insists on about a totally inappropriate market to go into; a crop of quality problems that stem from some unrest back on the shop floor stirred by a militant shop steward; a string of broken delivery promises caused by some inefficient work-scheduling by the production supervisors; a tactless letter from an accounts clerk about an overdue payment. He's the one in the firing line — not literally perhaps, but who else is?

To do the job at all, even to retain his sanity, that ability to cope is essential to him. To do the job *well* he needs an abundant supply of it. The best salesmen combine to an extraordinary degree the ability to show genuine interest in and sympathy for their customer's viewpoint (they are good listeners), and the inner strength to convince him that the deal the company is offering him is a fair one. The stress on them is vastly increased if they can't honestly believe that themselves.

Is it any wonder that so many others don't quite come up to the mark? That so many have to find excuses for their sales failures by criticising other facets of the company's marketing — *even when the company has got them right*? There isn't a salesman born who couldn't sell the thing if only its price were lower, or if only it had this extra feature or that, or if only we painted it purple-and-pink. An organisation can get itself into a mess if it treats every salesman as the ultimate authority on its product or its distribution or its promotion or its price. Certainly his ideas are worth listening to — but as ideas, not as marketing imperatives.

But to come back to the point. In many organisations there's simply no need for people other than the sales force ever to meet a real, live customer. The outfit could survive perfectly well without a single other person ever getting together with any of its customers — *any* of them, however they're described. Of course, staff talk to customers on the phone, they write them letters, but that's not at all the same thing. The real pressure is on when you can see the customer and he can see you. Think about it. If your company makes sausages or boxes of matches or clocks, is it absolutely necessary for *anyone* apart from the sales force ever to go out there and physically meet a wholesaler or retailer or member of the public that buys your thing? Would the company cease to function? No.

What about all those other organisations where their staff have *got* to meet customers? That's different! Take a hotel for instance. Receptionists, porters, barmen, waiters, night staff — all have continually to be in contact with customers in the act of doing their jobs, otherwise the place would have no 'product' to market. *They are themselves part of the product*: a key element in its 'craftsmanship' is their manner with guests. All of them share the kinds of pressure that in an industrial firm are solely on the salesman's shoulders. The business is a 'people business'.

And the same applies to many if not most businesses whose product is a *service*. Think of shops, banks, garages, travel or transport organisations, firms that service appliances at the customer's premises... Then start thinking about public services: post offices, hospitals, employment exchanges, social services departments... They are all 'people businesses' in one form or another.

Of all the facets of marketing we've looked at so far, if anything lets the product down in the eyes of the customers, this is it. Many, many of them haven't found out how to manage their staff so that *this* work is properly done — the work of showing to the customer a pleasant courtesy, an attitude that improves his regard for the organisation's offerings. The fact remains: THIS IS PART OF THE WORK ITSELF. It isn't something that's merely nice if you can get it, an attribute that can be tacked on as an after thought.

If an organisation has a problem in the way a part of its work is done, it has just three options:
- *live with the problem*: it can ignore it, trust it won't matter too much, hope it will go away of its own accord.
- *solve the problem*: it can try to improve the way the work is done.
- *avoid the problem*: it stops trying to do the thing at all (or at least reduces the amount of it that's done). It discovers a completely different way of achieving an acceptable end-result — acceptable to the customer in this case, of course.

**Living with the problem** is the most common response if an organisation has a weakness in the 'people' element of its marketing. It simply leaves the problem alone. It lets its staff go on damaging its reputation with its market and, without realising it, reducing the quality of its 'product'.

Often it's a business enterprise. And it pays a penalty. To compete with rivals whose staff *are* good with customers, it has to do more in the other facets of its marketing to compensate and hang on to its own customers. That costs money and effort. The rest of its product has to be made that much better. It may have to spend more on the product's promotion. Often it has to shave its profit margins to make its prices more competitive. The market is a tough place to be in, and the customer requires his pound of flesh of those companies whose staff don't treat him with reasonable civility.

It's a pity the same pressures don't often apply in public service. The majority seem to allow their staff to behave just as the mood takes them towards the unfortunate public that has to meet them. If they're surly or bossy or just plain rude, most organisations don't seem to *care*. The only pressure that exists is the individual's sense of duty to the people his institution is there to serve. Certainly there's little evidence of pressure from its management.

**Solving the problem** is usually easier said than done. A manager who thinks it's enough simply to tell his staff to behave nicely is being naïve. They might try when he's there, but as soon as his back is turned they'll slide back into the same old habits. And it's not their fault. Whatever the manager feels, *they* haven't the gut-feeling that it's really important. That's the feeling you've got to have to make the effort, moment by moment, hour by hour, day by day as you meet customers. They aren't all nice people to deal with, and a few can be really upsetting (though whether they'd be so unpleasant if they'd been treated the right way in the first place might be a moot point). If you're at the receiving end, it's hard to avoid reacting instinctively and emotionally. You have to keep reminding yourself that you personally are not the target. For many people who don't cope successfully, it's not because they won't. It's because they can't — not continuously, anyway. Being good with customers is a difficult art to learn.

If you're a manager in search of a solution to your staff's poor manner with customers you have to be prepared for a long haul. It's not enough to hope that your own example will do the trick. First you have to show that you care deeply about the end-result of your patch — the whole of it, not just the bit that you personally have a hand in: you have to give your people something they can take pride in. (They have to believe in the product before they can represent it well to the world outside.) If you can't do that, forget the whole thing.

Then you have to demonstrate your concern for the customers and your dissatisfaction with the way they are being treated. At the same time, you have to show understanding of your own people's difficulties with the customer. You have to discuss improvements with them, listen to their ideas, show them that for all your criticism of them you respect them as fellow human beings. You have to teach them, encourage them, support them, show recognition of their genuine achievements. Above all, you have yourself to learn not just how to manage work, but also how to Manage People.*

*Footnote : *Managing People* is the title of another book in this series.

**Avoiding the problem** is in fact the route a lot of organisations and even whole industries have taken — though its doubtful whether they would see its *main* purpose as reducing the people-problem in their marketing. *They construct the 'product' so that it involves less human contact with the customer:*

- the retail trade stops physically 'serving the customer' and lets the customer help himself. Supermarkets are the obvious example, but not the only one. Think of petrol-filling stations, DIY hardware shops, self-service carveries and cafeterias...
- hotels become what the trade calls 'minimum service hotels' (an unfortunate phrase, that!). There are no porters to carry your bags, if you want a drink in our room you use the kettle or mini-bar there rather than calling room service...
- a huge range of products are dispensed by vending machines rather than people: anything from photography booths to banks' cash-dispensing tills.
- direct mail order outfits sell to the customer at home by the catalogue, not by putting goods through the retail service industry at all. *They*'ve found a way to dispense even with the sales force!

Now the obvious purpose of all this is to reduce costs. In a service organisation, employees are expensive items — often the biggest of its outgoings. If the firm can design its service to reduce the number of people it needs around the place to deal with customers, it can provide the service more cheaply.

It might also be able to improve the 'product' in other ways: for example, widening the customer's range of choice, giving him a feeling of more control over what he's getting, extending the hours over which he can use the service. There might even be a hidden benefit in the fact that the customer isn't 'bothered' by its staff — meaning staff who can't handle the contact with him properly.

Two things to note: usually there has to be *someone* the customer meets at some point. If there's so little contact with him, the contacts that *do* exist become all the more important to handle right. And in many markets the customer prefers the contact, and will even pay more to get it. Perhaps supermarkets will never entirely put out of business those small stores that do have staff to meet their customer, who give him a cheery greeting and a feeling of genuine desire to help him.

# 5. 'Price'

## THE BUSINESS ORGANISATION:

### *What will our customer pay?*

When this last facet of marketing is mentioned, most people start thinking automatically about *money*. Some never get beyond that. It's the price-tag on the product, and the resulting flow of coins, banknotes, cheques and whatnot into the greedy coffers of business. Money is certainly involved — who can deny it? To the individual who thinks in a profit-centred way, it's *all* that's involved. But that leaves out a heap of important things.

To the market-centred organisation, this isn't what 'price' is really about. The point isn't money — which *by itself* doesn't mean anything at all. You can't eat it, wear it or live in it. It won't educate your children, transport you where you want to go or care for you when you're ill. The real point is **value.** The organisation and its people — particularly its sales force — have the knack of looking at whatever they are doing for the customer as *value to him*. They don't 'sell on price'. They offer 'value for money'.

The *businessman* (as opposed to the managers and other people who work in the organisation) has an extra knobble on the knack. He doesn't even think in terms of value for money. He asks for 'money for value' — and there's a difference. He doesn't start with the money and then say "let's see. Given that money, what value should we offer our customers?" He puts the question the other way round: "what money should we ask our customers to pay for the value we're providing them with?"

His special ability is one of *uprating in his own mind the value to the customers of whatever he's doing for them.* He looks at his product to see what he can justify to himself as its full value to the customer. He gives himself the confidence in that value to convince the customers too, and then to ask the price he reckons it deserves. Don't confuse this with the ability of the con-man to ask a price that *he knows* is way above the real value of the thing. The businessman starts with its value to the customer. Its price is the outcome of that value.

To decide its prices, the business organisation has to find the answers to these questions:

- how much money do we need?
- what is our customer willing to pay?
- how should we arrive at the price?
- how can we get the value we've earned?

## 1. How much money do we need?

The word is 'need', not 'want'. To survive at all, a firm needs a certain minimum level of income. To be healthy, it needs something above the minimum. The money is needed for four — and only four — different things:

- for **costs**: the money that goes to pay its own people, and the organisations outside who supply whatever it uses in doing its work.
- for **investors**: the money that's needed to pay back the shareholders and bankers or whoever has put up the money to get the firm started and to enable it to survive and grow.
- for **taxes**: the money that the State demands.
- for **reserves**: the money that needs to be put aside for the future. That's the money that will enable the firm to improve its 'product' — as it *must* do to hold on to its market.

In any organisation, its own costs are far and away the biggest of those money-users. They also happen to be the one that the organisation's managers can do most to control. And that doesn't mean solely top management. It depends on the concern of *every* manager — from top to bottom — for the economy of his own patch, and his skill in spotting things under his control that are wasting his organisation's resources:

- waste of materials and extravagant buying (which may mean cheap purchases that are buying trouble for the future).
- mis-use of equipment and space (it has got to be paid for).
- activities being done that don't need to be done.
- poor organisation that gets people working at cross-purposes, wasting each others' time and effort.

— planning failures that allow problems to crop up that ought not to happen.
  — badly-designed systems that absorb more time than their results are worth.
— mismanagement of people that leaves their capacities idle, or that fails to draw from them the effort and commitment they're capable of.

To control the organisation's costs effectively, every manager needs not only to manage the work and the people he's responsible for. Whether he's the Chief Executive or a supervisor, he needs also to understand what is involved in Managing Money inside his organisation.*

The prices an organisation *needs* to charge are a direct reflection of its own costs. But it's another question whether the customer is willing to pay a price that's inflated by the high costs of bad management.

## 2. What is our customer willing to pay?

This question runs straight back to the 'product' the organisation is providing for its customers: What is its *value* to them in terms of its design, its craftsmanship and its availability? How does that value compare with the value of the competing products?

You might object that this leaves out of the picture the question of what the customer can *afford*. But that's really a matter of deciding which customer the organisation is aiming for: the low-price market? Or the middle or upper price-bracket? Wherever it is pitching its product in the market-place, it's likely to find it has competitors pitching in the same place. Anyway, the customer's question "can I afford it?" isn't the complete question. It's really "do I want to afford *this* rather than some of the *other* things I could be spending my money on?" The firm is still competing on the value that he sees or can be persuaded to see in its product *compared with the value he sees in other things he could buy*.

True, an organisation has to know how 'price-sensitive' its market is. Not all customers are equally concerned about the exact price. Some do count the cost down to the last penny. Often they're at the cheap end of whatever market they're in, either by personal inclination or out of simple necessity. Never mind the value — they'll go for the lowest price they're offered. But most are more concerned about the value of the thing they're buying than about a price a pound or two above the prices or rivals who are offering poorer value.

Of course before he has actually bought it, a customer's idea of the value of the thing to him depends on what he's told

*Footnote: Managing Money is the title of another book in this series.

about it. It also depends on how clearly he has defined his own wants and needs. The company's advertising is there to do the first job, but it often can't succeed too well with the customer who's not sure what he wants. That's the prime job of the sales force — to help the customer focus his own interests sharply enough to see what really represents value to *him*.

What many manufacturing organisations overlook is the way their product's delivery affects its value to their customers. A thing that you can get *now* may be worth more to you than a better designed and crafted thing that you can't have for another month. The New York Federal Reserve Bank did a survey of different countries' export performance and the effects in overseas markets. It discovered that, in most cases a country delivering its products one month sooner than its rivals could charge a price 5% higher than theirs. You don't need export markets to prove that. Exactly the same thing applies in home markets too: quicker, more reliable delivery increases the value of the product and it can be priced accordingly. The interesting thing about the Bank's survey was the fact it could put a price on that value.

## 3. How should we arrive at the price?

Commercial organisations operate a variety of pricing methods of varying sophistication. But they all boil down to a choice between two approaches:

- cost-plus pricing.
- market pricing.

**Cost-plus pricing** sets the price by what it costs the organisation to provide the goods or service that it supplies to each customer. It charges him its own costs in serving him plus an extra margin — a 'gross profit' on each deal. The extra goes towards its overheads and paying its investors and all the other financial needs that it has.

It's a take-it-or-leave-it kind of pricing. The organisation doesn't particularly try to calculate what the customer is willing to pay. But if it's going to stay in business, it has to be at least as efficient as its rivals to keep its costs down.

**Market pricing** means that the orgnisation does it the other way round. It sets its prices by what the market is willing to pay, regardless of its own costs. So the prices depend on what the organisation reckons is the value of its product to the customer as compared with the value its competitors are offering. It may even be prepared to bargain with the customer.

Sometimes this may mean that the company is selling its products *below* what they cost it to produce. It might do this for just a few of a wide range of products — 'loss leaders' as they're called. Or it might do it for a short time over the whole of a range of products to break into a new market, or to send a competitor to the wall. Usually it can't continue doing this for long if it wants to avoid going bust itself! *How* long depends on its reserves of financial muscle.

But the opposite applies too: market-pricing may mean prices very much *higher* than the company's own costs. It charges 'what the market will bear'. If the market isn't price-sensitive, and if competitors are all offering poorer value, who's worried about massive profits? Once the costs and investors and taxes are all paid, the rest can go to make the company even stronger in the future, so everyone is happy except the competitors. It's up to them to get the value of *their* products up to scratch.

Actually, most organisations blend both approaches in their pricing policies. The prices that are set try to balance the organisation's need for income against what the customers will pay. Set the prices too high and there won't be any customers. Set them too low and there won't be enough income. So the organisation has to:
— forecast the level of business it expects to get (how busy does it expect to be?)
— calculate what prices will earn its keep at that level.
— look to see that the customers will not be put off by those prices (will they feel the product's value to them is worth its price?).
— look over at what the competitors are doing (will that affect the business forecast we started with?)

D'you want to read that again? Pricing is a ticklish business!

## 4. How can we get the value we've earned?
A company in a cash business has no problem here. It gets cash-on-the-nail for each transaction it does with a customer. The problem is for all those companies that don't have a cash business — the ones who give credit.

Giving credit is rather like the delivery question in reverse: the company has to wait for the money to be delivered. And just as a product that's delivered late to a customer is worth less to *him*, so a payment delivered late to the company is worth less to *it*. A pound in a month's time isn't worth quite as much as a pound now. If it's in the customer's bank account for that time, it's increasing the value of the deal he's getting: that becomes part of the total value that has to be taken into account in the company's pricing — whichever method it chooses.

This makes **credit control** a very important part of the organisation's work. If it's getting all its invoices paid an average of say three months after it has sent them out, that's a quarter of a year's total income *permanently* missing. The result may be that it's starved of the funds it needs for survival and health, the money it has *got* to have to pay its costs, its investors, its taxes and to put by for the future. *Something* has to give, and the company hasn't all that many options:

— it can try to hold down the amount of money it pays its people — its own workforce and managers. For a while they might accept it, but the company is storing up trouble for itself in the future.

— it can try to delay paying its suppliers. But that's reducing the value of the money they've earned, and they may not be prepared to accept it if they can find better business elsewhere. The company may lose some valuable sources of supply (Remember Konosuke Matsushita's four goals? One of them was "maintain good relations with suppliers".)

— it can try to borrow more money from investors. But if they know the company is in trouble they may either be unwilling to put up more money, or may demand a high rate of interest for the risk they're being asked to accept. So the company is crippled even further.

— it can mortgage its own future by 'eating the seed corn'. It dips into the reserves set aside for the necessary development of its 'product'. It may even sell off some of the resources (property or equipment) that it actually needs for *today's* product. That might either increase or reduce the product's value to the customers, and so the price they'll be willing to pay.

Whichever way it turns, the company is in trouble. And the trouble may not be solely the fault of its credit control. As often, it's the result of the failure of *all* its managers to control the company's costs: it simply can't provide the value the customer requires at a price he is prepared to pay. It *needs* too much money for its own good!

But where credit control *is* the problem, what can the company do? One thing is to look at the speed with which it sends out its invoices. Companies have been known that are on the breadline and are *still* sending their invoices out three to four months late, would you believe.

The second thing is to look at the way the company chases up the late payers among its customers. Often a company will leave this vital work to its credit control clerks. But they aren't usually equipped with the people-skills to persuade the customer to pay up without risking the loss of his future business. Remember, the point of the organisation's purpose — 'to create customers' — is that the organisation *keeps* them as customers. It can neither afford to give free loans because its clerks aren't persuasive enough, not to lose a customer simply because of an offensive letter or telephone call.

The answer is not to leave it to the credit control clerks. It's a job that demands the special skills of the salesman. And don't go saying "but our salesmen are there to *sell*, not to act as debt-collectors". Selling includes seeing that the money comes in, otherwise your sales force is acting as a Father Christmas to your customers. Of course, a lot can be done with a series of good chasing letters (but *good* chasing letters, not the kind of distant, formal or threatening missives so many organisations seem to use). If they don't do the trick, it's the salesman's job to go in there and charm the customers into paying. *He* has the skills — *and* the relationship with each customer — to do it.

There's a third thing the company can do: avoid getting hitched up with non-customers — because that's what non-payers actually are. A customer is someone who pays. A non-customer is someone who'll take your product and then — you can go whistle for your money! If the sales force sell to people who can't or won't pay, they're *not* 'creating customers'. They're just increasing the organisation's costs. Part of the skill of the really able salesman is in his ability to sniff out the doubtful credit-risks *without upsetting the sound customers*, and then to get someone in credit control to do a check on their credit-worthiness.

The organisation that really has the problem sewn up is the one that persuades the customers to *pay in advance*. Then the customer is carrying the credit risk, and the money he pays is worth *more* than it's worth when he actually receives the 'product'. Just as money that's paid late is worth less, so money that's paid in advance is worth more. For the company, it's like having your cake and eating it. Whole industries and services are run this way (you can only do it if *all* your competitors are doing it too, or if your prices are well below theirs). Think of the holiday industry. Think of insurance companies. Think of private schools. Think of the travellers' cheques you buy from your bank: what you're buying isn't the bits of paper. It's the service your bank performs when it honours the cheques. Across banks as a whole, that's an average of six weeks after they've been paid for. It's cash-in-advance, though a lot of people don't realise it.

Now all this kind of thinking ought to be second nature to any manager in a business organisation. But what about managers in public service — in the civil service, national health, local government...?

## THE PUBLIC SERVICE ORGANISATION

*What will our 'customer' pay — indirectly?*

So? Let's go over the four questions again to see what's different:

## 1. How much money do we need?

Your organisation has to pay **tax** in *some* form. It surely needs **reserves**. It may also have **investors** from whom it has borrowed money that has to be paid back. And it certainly has **costs**. Have another look at the paragraphs about them — and particularly at the list of money-wasters. Every one of them applies in public service. That's where a lot of the damned money is going, and that's one important reason why the customers aren't happy.

## 2. What is our customer willing to pay?

The market doesn't have any choice in the matter. And anyway, you don't have any competitors with whom the customers could compare the value of the 'product' your organisation provides. That doesn't remove the need to consider its **value** — *and its value as the customers see it.* It puts a duty of honour on you and all your colleagues in the outfit to make sure that its 'product' *is* properly designed and crafted for them to the fullest extent that its income allows, and that the public is properly informed about what's going on. We all have a right to see what value we're getting from the public services we pay our rates and taxes for.

## 3. How should we arrive at the price?

Your organisation has no choice here. Its charge to the public purse is a **cost price** — and the cost itself is partly regulated by the amount of money the Government of the day makes available. If the money is restricted, you're back to the cost-and-value problem again: what is the best value the organisation *can* produce with the money it has available to spend?

## 4. How can we get the value we've earned?

Your organisation doesn't usually have to worry. That's most often for the public to worry about, because *they pay in advance.*

The thing that's often supposed to separate business from public service is 'profit'. We've tried to show it's not. Profit isn't needed as an explanation of what business does. Nor does it help to say that public service doesn't need to 'sell' its products. It has to be concerned with what the public thinks of them. Even the police, when they realise they have problems with their public image, try to do something about it. What's that if it's not 'selling the service to the public'?

The real distinction is *competition*. In a business, wherever you're working, your work is competing with the work of your opposite numbers in other businesses in the same field. It's not just for the sales force to worry about out there meeting the competition head on. They can only sell what they're given to sell — and that's the end-result of your work, your people's work, and the work of every last body in the place.

If your outfit is a public service, it's different. It doesn't have to compete to stay in existence — not in the day-to-day sense that applies in business. A lot of public administration couldn't operate competitively anyway: an authority can't have rivals unless you've got a Revolution in progress. But the purpose still remains. And if the gulf between the costs and the value produced yawns too widely, even a public body can find itself under pressure eventually.

## ... and back to work

If you're the manager of an important function, the connection is obvious. Your department is there among the facets of marketing we've described, along with those of all your managerial peers. But that isn't the sole point. The extent to which you all share a single-minded purpose in the market-place has to be a crucial question for the organisation you all serve. It's a purpose that often suffers a multiple fracture. Each managerial baron claims the priority for his own function and downrates the importance of the others — sometimes unwittingly even torpedoes their contributions. A house divided against itself, according to Biblical observation, cannot stand. Anyhow, it can't successfully market itself and its offerings. In the map we've presented, the routes towards collaboration should be clear.

And if you're 'only' a supervisor? The whole of this explanation has really been for you. Too often, you and your people are held not to have the capacity or interest to understand things like these. We've tried to show that marketing is no great mystery. Its basics are marvellously simple. Indeed, sometimes the people in a workforce understand its essential point in their work better than their so-called management does. The only 'marketing' done in such organisations is performed by the other ranks, not by the officers. In a real sense, the 'top management' is coming from the bottom.

When your superiors really do see their purpose as marketing, you have many opportunities to make an intelligent contribution. To grasp them, you need to be able to share that market view. Where else can you get a sense of direction for the decisions *you* make? So for you the map is intended as a guide to the way you might try to make yourself better informed:

*about your organisation*
- what is it attempting to do in the market-place?
- how important does that make each of its various operations?
- what gains customers for it? What keeps them? What loses them?
- what are its strengths and weaknesses in the different facets of its marketing (compared with rivals if it has them)?

*about the work you manage*
- how does it contribute? What effects can it have for good or ill on your organisation's 'product', 'place', 'promotion', 'public information', 'people', 'price'?
- is anything on your patch causing harm to any of those aspects of marketing? What can you do about it? Where can you get advice or help — from your boss? From colleagues? From your people?
- how can you shape your actions and decisions towards constructive ends out in the market place?
- how can you encourage your people to share your views? Where could *they* contribute more effectively?

As a supervisor you have a key role to play in your organisation's marketing, so it's not unreasonable to expect you to know what's involved in it altogether. Who else in management stands closer to the real 'product' than you? Who has a better day-by-day control over the quality the customer actually gets? And who is better able to give your people a clear sense of the PURPOSE which their work should aim to achieve?

# The purpose of the organisation

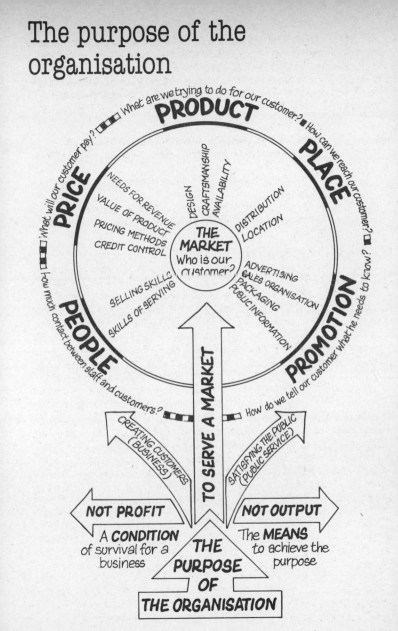

# 4. Getting things organised

Whatever your management job, you can't do it properly without some skill in organising people's activities. True, the scope for using your abilities in this direction does rather depend on your level. If you're a senior manager, some of the biggest decisions you can make are about the structuring of your total department or division. If you're a supervisor your scope is restricted. But you still need to understand what's involved in organising — for two reasons:

— you are bound to have *some* responsibility for arranging and allocating work. As a manager you can't duck all the blame if things get into a mess.

— you have to work within the framework that's created by your superiors' decisions. You can do that better if you know how the system operates and what freedom of action it gives you.

If you're *not* aware of what's involved, you'll often fail to realise how you could be making your patch more efficient. And it's even more unlikely you'll be able to persuade your boss to see where *his* action is needed to cure more fundamental weaknesses that are wasting time and resources. You might even get to thinking that the problems they cause are somehow inevitable.

A manager organises work in several different ways. There's the way he defines his people's jobs — not always explicitly perhaps, but in any case by the work he allocates to them, the instructions he gives them, the way he controls what they do. There's his method of dividing responsibilities between the different jobs. There are the procedures he sets up for getting things done. There are the communication channels he uses to coordinate the activities on his patch with what goes on elsewhere in the organisation.

The starting point is his understanding of what a 'job' actually means. It's what often causes problems. Many managers simply don't have a clear way of defining the work each person does in an organisation. Not the fact that it means doing things, being active, using effort, exercising abilities. That's obvious. What's missing is an insight into what actually shapes a job. So this is where we begin.

# A. What is a job?

A job isn't simply what someone does. To define it adequately, you also have to consider what he's supposed to look after and the pressure system within which he works. besides that, there's the question of what he *shouldn't* do and why not.

Every job has a basic framework that's governed by three things. Take your own job for instance. Some of the work is done because you've no other option — those are the things you're forced to do by the orders you have to obey: they are the *demands* of your job. Other work you do because that's the way you see your job — the things you do out of choice or habit: they are your way of satisfying the *responsibilities* of your job. But you are limited in your freedom to choose how you do this work: you have to operate within the *boundaries* created by the organisation's rules. Whatever job you do, it's bound to be shaped like this:

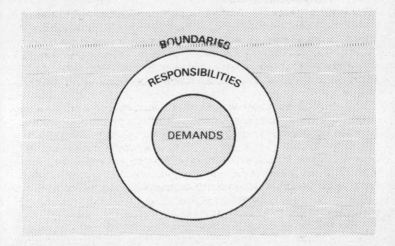

**Demands** are whatever you do simply in response to instructions or because a system makes you do them. They are the tasks you're told to carry out, the deadlines you're ordered to meet, the methods you've got to use, the procedures you must follow. Together they make up an irreducible minimum that anyone in your job would have to do simply to stay there.

If you don't comply with each of the demands in your job, you're guilty of either negligence or insubordination — it's a disciplinary matter. If you do comply and the fact you've done so causes a problem, your superiors can't hold you responsible.

You were simply doing as you were told. On the other hand, you earn no medals simply for fulfilling your job's demands.

In this sense, the demands of your job aren't what the common phrase means — the stresses and strains it creates for you, the difficulties you have to cope with. Nor are they necessarily what you might see as your most important activities (the 'key tasks' in a job description perhaps). Managers often think their day is filled with demands, with things they've got to attend to there and then. But if they were really to question themselves about what they are doing and the way they use their time, they'd find that often they're being ruled by their own habits, not by demands. Nearly always they've got a choice — for instance whether to postpone action on something that has just arisen, or whether to delegate some work they've got used to doing themselves. With demands there are no choices.

**Responsibilities** are the parts of the job where you're free to choose what you do or how you do it. You have scope to use your initiative, take your own decisions, even delegate the decision-making where you feel that's sensible. If the decisions are bad or you duck making them, you may be criticised for being ineffective, but you can't be accused of insubordination: poor judgement isn't a disciplinary offence. On the other hand, this *is* how you're performance is reckoned — by the quality of the judgement you use in fulfilling your responsibilities.

A single task often contains both demands and

responsibilities. For instance, a manager may instruct his staff to give him regular weekly reports on their activities. He requires that the reports are on his desk by four o' clock on Friday and that they're laid out in a certain way. These are his demands. But what his staff put into their reports is their responsibility. If the reports are completed on time but are poorly written he may criticise his staff's lack of skill or care, but he can't discipline them for disobedience. If their rigid adherence to the layout makes the reports muddled and incomplete he might complain about their poor judgement, but he can't accuse them of insubordination. If they spend too long on the report-writing and skimp their work on something else he may be dissatisfied with their time-allocation, but they're not guilty of negligence.

*Every* job contains responsibilities. In the real world you won't find a job that consists of nothing but demands. Some people might think a job like a filing clerk's, for example, is just routine — but they're wrong. Even he has to use his judgement at times:

- if he gets several requests for filed information at the same time, which should he satisfy first?
- if he becomes overloaded with work, should he let a temporary backlog build up or ask his supervisor for assistance?
- if a document could be put in more than one place in the system, how should he file it?
- if he has an idea about a more efficient method of working, how should he implement it?

However exactly his work is specified, it's impossible to remove all *responsibility* from it.

Of course, how much of anyone's work stems from responsibilities and how much from demands varies from job to job. More than anything else it depends on the *level* of the job in the organisation. The filing clerk's job has limited responsibilities but many demands. The chief executive's job is the reverse — wide responsibilities and few absolute demands. Even among people who are nominally doing the same kind of work, the scope of their responsibilities varies. For instance, you might have a group of people who all work to the same job description. In practice you and they know the jobs are different. You give different people work of varying difficulty and responsibility according to your confidence in the ability of each one to use good judgement, to make wise decisions. The *demands* in the job may all be the same; the *responsibilities* differ.

Responsibilities always give scope for choice. But this doesn't mean that people actually choose how to handle them. Their actions are often governed by habit — they get used to doing things in certain ways they feel comfortable with. They may even convince themselves they must act in this or that way, that they have no alternative. But the scope is there all the same, and it'll be seen differently by different people with the same responsibilities. It gives each person the opportunity to make his own decisions about how to shape the role he performs. Whether he *uses* the opportunity wisely is another matter.

**Boundaries** are the things that limit your freedom of action on your responsibilities. They are created in various ways:

— many are set by the *policies* decided by managers above you in the organisation: things like organisation structure, work requirements, budgets, spending limits, hours of attendance, overtime restrictions, disciplinary rules and procedures, union agreements and so on.

— the way your boss *delegates* to you creates further important boundaries — the amount of authority he gives you, where he draws the line on what you can and can't decide on you own, the kinds of things he checks up on.

— there are *practical considerations* that limit what you can do: the capabilities of your people, how they respond to your management of them, the physical resources you have available, the behaviour that's expected of you, even the way your colleagues and superiors organise *their* work.

Taken together, the boundaries determine what you can and cannot do on your own authority.

Some of a job's boundaries are disciplinary matters just like its demands are. If you ignore a policy or consistently overstep your authority, you can be accused of insubordination and may run the risk of being removed from your job. But other boundaries are simply questions of what is and isn't possible. And just like the responsibilities, they'll be seen differently by different people in the same job. What one manager deems a sheer impossibility may be achieved perfectly well by his successor in his post. In fact, among the choices your responsibilities give you is whether to test the boundaries to see if they are as fixed as you suppose.

There's an important point to understand about the way instructions and policies shape people's jobs throughout an organisation. Every manager is making decisions about these things in two different ways. Some of them apply only to the people who report directly to him: these are the decisions he takes on the work of his subordinates in his **immediate command**. Others apply to *their* subordinates too and even to people below them, right down to the lowest levels of his part of the organisation: these are his decisions that are binding on people throughout his **extended command**. There's a big difference between the two. The first kind create demands on his immediate subordinates, but don't necesarily limit their responsibilities. The second kind redraw the boundaries of their jobs — they lose some of their freedom of action on their responsibilities.

Take an example. A plant manager in charge of a factory has several superintendents reporting to him. In turn, each superintendent has below him a number of foremen who supervise the workforce. Suppose the manager is worried about an increase in the number of rejects among the products being made, and wants to give instructions to reduce the wastage. He can do this in two ways:

1.     He can instruct his superintendents to investigate the reasons for rejects. They are to present reports in four weeks' time giving the causes they've discovered, what they have done to overcome them, and their recommendations on any further action which is beyond their authority to take.

        This is an instruction within the manager's IMMEDIATE COMMAND only — the superintendents. It creates a *demand* on them to do the investigation and to report by the time specified. But it leaves them entirely *responsible* for deciding how to tackle the problem — even whether or not to delegate some of the work to the foremen.

2.     He can also require his superintendents to instruct each foreman to list every operation in his sections that has produced more than (say) 4% rejects over the past three months. The sources of scrap are to be analysed according to the operatives, machines, processes and materials involved. Any foreman who can't cope is to ask for help through his superintendent from the production engineering department.

        This now becomes an instruction to the manager's **extended command** — it includes the foremen in its demands. By doing this it creates new **boundaries** that greatly restrict the superintendents' freedom of action. It limits their responsibility for making their decisions on how to tackle the problem.

So this enables us to draw a picture of the way that managers' decisions and policies operate throughout an organisation. In this picture, the triangles are the decisions made by managers at each level that apply only to their immediate command; the circles are their decisions that affect their extended command.

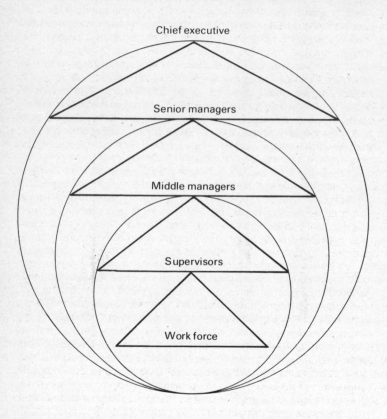

This is what actually happens in every organisation, not merely what's supposed to happen. An organisation can't work any other way. At every level, managers are establishing policies and giving instructions not only for their immediate command but also for their extended command. At every level, the scope of each manager's responsibilities is bounded by the decisions of managers at all the levels above him from the top of the organisation down. Policy-making isn't restricted to senior managers. It's something *every* manager is doing in one way or another.

The trouble is that managers often don't define their policies clearly — particularly the ones they make for their extended command. In the levels below them, other managers are left in doubt about what they are actually responsible for, the boundaries within which they have to work. Sometimes they can't even be certain about the demands on them. In really bad cases, no one can be sure what decisions he or anyone else is authorised to make. Every time an individual faces a problem, he first has to think: "am I or aren't I responsible for dealing with this?" Before deciding what to do about it, he has to decide whether it's up to him to do anything — or whether other people would see that as usurping *their* authority. Will his boss bawl him out or praise him for showing initiative? If jobs don't have clear boundaries, no one knows in advance which response he'll get.

Decision-making is always difficult because of its uncertainties. There's always a lapse of time before you know whether or not your decision was a good one. But if you're constantly being judged not only on how you decided to deal with a problem but also on whether you were right to assume the problem was yours to deal with, life becomes intolerable. You're in a state of constant doubt about what your job actually is. That's bound to affect how well you do it. Also in that kind of situation there are endless possibilities for people to play politics.

There's another snag when policies and delegation of authority are left unclear. It makes change difficult if not impossible to implement properly. Changes in the way things are done in an organisation always involve changes to existing policy. But if policies aren't defined in the first place, it's very hard to spell out how they are going to be changed. For example, suppose a manager faces a steady and worrying rise in the amount his area spends on certain supplies. He wants to stop the increase and eventually get the spending back to an acceptable level. But he has never tried to define policy on the subject before, so he doesn't know which of his people are making the various decisions that cause the expense. The first thing he has to do is establish which jobs have the responsibility for decisions that affect the use of the supplies. In other words, before you can change anything in the future, you have to get quite clear how the *present* policy operates.

Suppose the manager doesn't do this and instead relies on his assumptions about who's responsible for his costs. He's quite likely to be wrong. Then the changes he tries to implement won't work either, and his subordinates may become anxious and resentful about them. He might think they're obstinate and resistant to change when actually they're concerned about the operational folly of the way he's tackling the problem. This isn't to suggest there's no such thing as genuine resistance to change. But it's often the result of managers trying to change things without a good understanding of how they're arranged at present. It's an organisational problem rather than a people problem.

All of this explains why managers need to get policies clearly stated — preferably in writing. The policies they're deciding for the people below them should be clear; the policies they themselves have to work within should be clear — the policies decided at higher levels. But many managers feel it is bad to formalise people's work like this. They argue that each person should be encouraged to take on as much responsibility as he can handle, and that their more able people would be prevented from doing so if they had to work within the boundaries of defined policies and specified authority. It's an unreal argument. In practice, every job always *has* got constraints surrounding it. The only question is whether they're stated or whether people are left to find them out by trial and error.

In any case, there always is freedom to make decisons *within* the boundaries. If they're uncertain about where the limits lie, *people can't feel free to act.* Without a clearly-defined area of freedom there is no real freedom. Clear policy statements and definitions of authority enable people to size up the scope of their responsibilities — the scope they have to shape their jobs for themselves, to choose how they fulfil their responsibilities.

In management jobs particularly, there's nearly always a choice of *emphasis.* Your own job for instance gives you choice over how you organise your time, choices over what you do with it. Some managers choose to spend more time on administration, others devote more time to their people. Some managers occupy themselves with DIY work, others delegate it to give more attention to their longer-term responsibilities. Sometimes the choice is even wider than this — managers in jobs with the same job title may do *totally different work.* A hotel manager's job is rather like this — different people play it in entirely different ways:

> — one spends his time in his office attending to paperwork and the administrative systems of his hotel. The returns he sends to Head Office show good cost-control and profitability. But he may be unaware of a lot of the things actually going on in his hotel, and may know few of the customers. He relies on his staff to tell him what he needs to know.

> — another concentrates on fostering business contacts. He knows all the influential people in the locality and spends a lot of time out and about. He's frequently in the restaurant or bars of his hotel — usually in the company of important guests. He trusts his staff to do the backstage work.

> — another is constantly around his hotel and has an eagle eye for every aspect of its operation down to the smallest detail. The standards he expects of his staff are high. Frequently he takes over himself if they can't cope or if their work isn't up to his exacting requirements.

> — yet another balances the attention he gives to cost controls, customers, the standards of his hotel. He runs it by delegation. He has good people in all the key posts and gives them considerable freedom. But he also insists they perform and is quick to find out if they don't. They are his first priority — their morale, their abilities, their training, the results they achieve.

Although they all have nominally the same job — even the same job-descriptions — these four managers choose to do very different work. Yet in a large hotel group, the same demands and constraints may apply to all of them, and their performance may be equally well regarded by their superiors.

True, a lot of management jobs may not give this scope — particularly at the lower levels in an organisation. But there are always *some* choices to be made. If you feel you have no choice about the way you deal with your responsibilities, stop and think for a moment: someone else in your job would handle them differently. He would see some things as more important than you do, other things as less important. He wouldn't arrange his time the same way. He might even spend time on tasks that you don't see as part of the job. If you look at your job this way, you'll probably find it has more possibilities than you'd thought. The boundaries that limit what you do may be the habits you've developed over the years rather than the policies of your superiors. You might even discover that the demands that seem to fill your day are partly caused by poor organisation of your work.

And the same for your people. The inadequacies of their performance may be due more to the way they interpret their jobs than to their lack of ability of commitment. Few people stand back to think about the different and perhaps better ways they could handle their roles. Understanding the choices they've got can help them to become more effective; it can also make their jobs more interesting for them. They can get more job satisfaction if they can see the scope for using their initiative.

Let's get down to practicalities. What does all this mean for you in your job as a manager? In the first place is suggests there ought to be a **job description** for each job in the area you command. This in turn requires some way of looking at how the work as a whole is divided up — a way of showing how the jobs fit together in a **structure diagram** of your part of the organisation. Then there are the policies and systems that regulate what is done — have they been written down? Do you have simple, clear **policy statements** and **system charts** so that everyone knows what they are, and you can consider whether they're adequate?

Perhaps you feel it isn't your job to concern yourself with things like these. In that case, what *is* your responsibility for organising the work in your area? Do you manage your patch or just cope with things as they happen? Are you a manager — or merely a minder?


# B. Job descriptions

Many managers don't see much point in written job descriptions. It's true of course that a job is really defined in people's heads, not on a sheet of paper. It's the way someone's work is understood by different people: by the person himself, by his boss, by other people his job brings him into contact with — including his subordinates. The job description is an attempt to bring together and pin down these understandings. But is the result worth the time and effort involved?

The truthful answer is often 'no'. But that's usually the fault of the way the job description has been prepared. If one exists for your job, does it really define the job as you know it to be?

Perhaps it's too vague and generalised. It might miss out important aspects of your work. On the other hand it may say you're responsible for things you know you're *not* solely responsible for. And it's more than likely it doesn't give much of a clue about the job's demands and boundaries. If it was prepared a few years ago, its probably more of a historical archive than a statement of the current state of affairs.

Perhaps this doesn't matter as far as you're concerned. You know your job and you get on with it. *But you're not the only person concerned.* What you do affects what others do in their jobs — the people who work alongside you, those above and below you in the organisation, even people in other sections and departments. And the same is true for your subordinates. If you're all to work together effectively, everyone needs a reasonable understanding of who's making decisions about what and where the limits of each job lie.

There *is* a need to define these things on paper to ensure that there's a common understanding of the basic framework. But it's not worth trying to spell out every detail of each person's work. Jobs change their shape with time: situations alter, policies are redefined, new instructions are given, tasks come and go. What's needed is a type of description that's accurate enough on the essentials of each job, but simple enough to be easily updated.

For anyone whose job includes some management, this means a form of job description that defines four main features of his role. Your job for instance can be defined in these terms:

## 1. Your command

What do you control — the people and the physical resources of property, equipment and materials in your patch of the organisation? What is the nature of the work it does? Does it have any special features you have constantly to be aware of, problems or possibilities that create priorities for your attention?

## 2. Demands

What have you personally got to do? What systems must you operate? What kinds of instruction must you obey — or at least, what are the sources of such instructions? Essentially, what actions could come to a disciplinary matter if you didn't take them?

## 3. Responsibilities

What aspects of the work within your area of command can you make your own decisions about, use your own judgement on? What are you responsible for with the people you command? What duty is placed on you to look after the economy and security of your patch? Where is it up to you to coordinate activities in your area with what is going on elsewhere?

## 4. Boundaries

Where are the limits that define your freedom of action on your resonsibilities? What kinds of policy must you observe? What are the limits of your authority to decide things for ourself? What are the major practical constraints you have to work within?

This doesn't necessarily mean a very long or involved kind of document — though it probably *is* more specific than the job description you've got at the moment. The idea is a set of *simple* statements that define the *key* features of the job you do.

To see what this kind of description might look like, suppose one has been written for the job of a Production Superintendent in an assembly shop;

## JOB DESCRIPTION

Production Superintendent　　　　　　　Date prepared:
Assembly Shop, ABC Factory.　　　　　June 19XX

## 1. Command

> — seven immediate subordinates (five supervisors, a production controller and a quality inspector). In his extended command are 48 assembly workers and three production control clerks.

- an area of 1000 sq. yds. of factory space containing assembly equipment, jigs, tools, conveyors and hoists.
- the work of assembling a range of XYZ products according to weekly programmes set by the Plant Manager. These give the number of each product type required and dates by which they are to be delivered to finished goods stores. Quality standards are specified for each type. The work requires careful handling of certain electrical components, and close liaison with manufacturing and product design to prevent problems with work flow or assembly techniques.

## 2. Demands

- implement each weekly programme received, or immediately report to the Plant Manager any difficulties in doing so.
- discuss problems raised by immediate subordinates. Decide action on operational difficulties that are interrupting work flow or are causing sub-standard quality.
- maintain these systems:
    - production planning and control.
    - costing and cost control.
    - performance records.
    - equipment reports.
    - staff timesheets.
    - analysis of expenditures.
- act immediately on any dangerous practices in the area.
- act on serious or persistent failure to comply with the company's code of discipline.
- attend the weekly production meeting.
- respond to instructions received from the Plant Manager.

## 3. Responsibilities

- allocate work to subordinates. This involves decisions on the workloads of their areas and the amount of authority to delegate to them. It also involves judgement on their effectiveness and, if unsatisfactory, taking action to correct the situation.
- decide in the light of the given work programmes what

supplies to requisition, what jigs and tools to order, what level of overtime to allow, and how to arrange for plant maintenance. If in his judgement existing resources are inadequate he is responsible for requesting extra resources from the Plant Manager.

— maintain the safety, discipline and morale of his entire workforce. This includes their selection, training and job placement. It also includes the handling of relationships with the union representatives in his area.

— keep all expenses under his control at the lowest level that is consistent with fulfilling his other responsibilities.

— decide any changes in working methods and in the use of his resources to improve output or quality, to speed the workflow, or to reduce the expenditure of material or time.

— recommend any changes in the organisation of his area or in its systems or staffing to improve its effectiveness. Also recommend modifications in product design to enable more efficient assembly.

## 4. Boundaries

— manpower available and departmental structure.

— physical resources allocated to the area.

— coordination requirements with these departments: Design, Supplies, Manufacturing, and Engineering.

— company policies: recruitment and promotion, pay scales, attendence, working conditions, union relationships, safety regulations etc.

— departmental policies: production techniques, quality standards, overtime, plant maintenance, security.

— budget established for the area's operations.

This kind of job description may be rather more detailed than many that exist. But do you see the advantage of spelling things out in this way — both of you and your people? Once it's done, you each know where you stand.

Test it for yourself. Try defining your job overleaf within the same sort of framework.

When you have done this, what about your subordinates' jobs? It is often revealing to extend the exercise to them (if they don't themselves have management responsibilities, you might find that the 'Command' element can be dropped). Better still, get *them* to define their jobs like this — and use the results to work out with them what their jobs *ought* to be. You get several benefits from this approach:

  — it focuses your thinking on how *work* is organised in your area. Much of the time we get this confused with people's temperaments, abilities, what they're good at. Defining the demands, responsibilities and boundaries of each job pushes you to concentrate on the work itself and the sort of job you want done.

  — it sets your people thinking about their jobs and why they tackle them in the way they do.

  — it shows where there are misunderstandings to be resolved about the different jobs. You discover the issues you have to discuss with each of your people.

  — it can help to determine who *ought* to be taking what decisions and where you might delegate more.

Besides these things, there is often a lot to be gained from looking at the jobs throughout a whole section or area. Sometimes it can reveal the scope for a more radical re-thinking of the way the whole operation is set up. If so, there's another kind of organisational tool that's also useful — diagrams that show the relationships between the jobs in a visual form...

## C. Structure Diagrams

A structure diagram is a way of picturing an organisation. Earlier you saw this example of the box-and-line arrangement that's usually used. Let's look at it in more detail now and talk about what you *can* read from the diagram and what you *can't*:

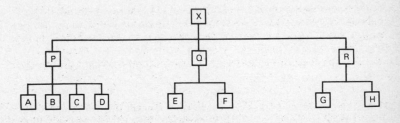

97

## JOB DESCRIPTION

Job Title: ...................................     Date ........................
...................................

### 1. Your command

_____

### 2. Demands

_____

# 3. Responsibilities

# 4. Boundaries

## What the diagram shows

X  Each box is a JOB, a set of *demands* and *responsibilities* for one person on duty in the organisation. You could think of it as representing the kind of job description you've just been drawing up.

The letter represents the JOB TITLE — *not* a person's name or grade. It's a common mistake to think the whole diagram is a picture of how people are arranged, and then to start trying to show their status by placing the boxes higher or lower on the paper. That misses the essential point of an organisation's structure: it ought to grow out of the *logic of the work*, not from the characteristics of the people. That should be obvious but often isn't. Many a structure seems to have been shaped more to accommodate personalities past or present than to make the work itself efficient.

Certainly a structure has to be adjusted to suit the abilities and characteristics of the people actually there, but *first* it has to be properly engineered for the work. It needs a logical base that won't be disrupted by changes in its membership. That base is what the diagram represents.

The levels of the boxes show differences only in the levels of responsibility. X is a set of bigger, longer-term responsibilities than those of P, Q and R — and theirs in turn are wider than those of A, B, C etc. The responsibilities of X encompass *all* the work of the lower-level boxes; the responsibilities of P embrace everything that's done in the A, B, C and D jobs.

Each line connecting a higher and lower level box is a line of FORMAL COMMUNICATION. It represents traffic moving in two different directions:

> downwards it is a line of AUTHORITY — communication to do with policy-making, order-giving and delegation. X gives instructions and delegates to P for instance, but not directly to A, B, C or D (unless he is *by-passing* P, which is something we'll come to in a moment).

> upwards it is a line of ACCOUNTABILITY — communication to do with the way demands have been fulfilled, policies maintained and delegated authority used. A, B, C and D are all accountable to P, not to X.

## What the diagram does not show

> You can't assume that only twelve people are involved. True, *at any one time* only twelve people are there. But the jobs represented by the dozen boxes might be done by twice as many people working different duty periods.

> In a shift operation working around the clock, the structure and even the work itself might change from period to period. In that case, two or three different diagrams may be needed to show what's actually happening.

> You can't assume who deputises for the person in job X. If he is away, he might arrange for any one of the people in jobs P, Q or R to stand in for him — or someone from elsewhere in the organisation beyond for that matter, even his own boss.

> You can't assume the people in jobs P, Q, and R have the same grade or status. You can't assume they have equivalent levels of responsibility either. Q may have a big special responsibility and considerable freedom of action. P's responsibilities may be far more limited by the demands and constraints of the job.

The diagram says nothing about the INFORMAL COMMUNICATION that's needed among the people involved. The people in jobs D and E may well talk to each other — and to R, and even X. The lines don't represent that sort of communication — getting and giving information, discussing things, working out ideas together, making requests or agreements etc.

All you can read from the diagram is that neither X nor R have the authority to give orders to D or E. X hasn't because it has been delegated to P (for D) and Q (for E); R hasn't because they aren't his subordinates anyway, not even indirectly. But then, nor can D decide things with E that are beyond the authority P and Q have delegated to them.

In real life, you can't assume that the person in X doesn't bypass the people in P, Q and R to give instructions direct to their subordinates. Sometimes he may have to do this — in their absence for instance. Sometimes the subordinates may bypass in the other direction, going to X for decisions etc. Occasionally this may be a reasonable thing to do in the interests of efficiency. It may not do any harm to P, Q or R's positions as long as they establish a rule: whenever it's done, their people are to inform them about it at the first opportunity. In that way, they still maintain their people's accountability to them.

But if it happens often, without good cause and with important areas of P, Q and R's responsibilities, it distorts the organisation. The structure actually becomes this:

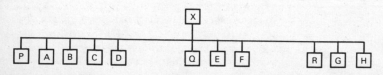

At this point, you might try drawing a structure diagram for your own organisation. Not the whole organisation if it's one of some size: It will be enough if you draw just the part of it you're directly involved in — your department or branch perhaps. At a bare minimum you should include the jobs of your boss, your colleagues (i.e. everyone else who reports to your boss) and those in your command — your subordinates and their subordinates down the line. If your job also gives you frequent contacts with people in your colleagues' command, you might well include their jobs too. Although the diagram doesn't actually represent the lines of informal communication, it can provide a useful basis for thinking about their implications.

If the diagram isn't too large, you might be able to develop it from the skeleton outline on the page opposite.

**Structure diagram for your area of the organisation**

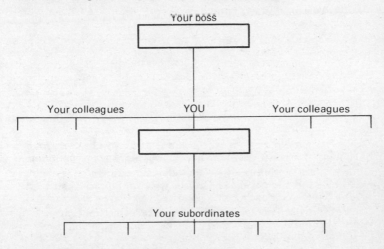

The point of drawing up such diagrams is twofold. In the first place they are useful for giving people an idea of how different parts of the organisation operate: in this sense they are information tools. It's a common management assumption that people don't need to know this sort of stuff, or that if they've been in the place for a while they get to know it anyway. That places an extraordinary faith in people's powers of intuition and

103

mind-reading. It's hardly surprising that many have gross misconceptions of how the different parts of their organisations function — even parts that connect quite closely with their own work. Still more common is uncertainty or just plain ignorance. They don't know how others are affected by their performance of their work, so why should they worry? Of course, structure diagrams by themselves don't explain what goes on, but they make a good starting point for informing people better about the organisation and how their own jobs fit into it.

The other purpose of drawing a diagram is to help managers think through the implications of their organisation structure. They are an aid in identifying weaknesses and thinking out possible improvements. If you can 'see' the way things are organised, it becomes easier to spot any symptoms of organisational rickets:

**Multiple masters**: is there anyone in your part of the organisation whose job would be shown like A in this diagram?

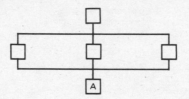

Then he has too many bosses — two too many in fact. He *might* be having to cope with uncoordinated and even conflicting demands, although that does depend on how reasonable each of his three superiors are and how well they harmonise their work. He *can't* rely on that and you *shouldn't*.

Better to see his job as providing a *service* to the three (i.e. informal communication), and make him formally *accountable* to just one person — perhaps like this:

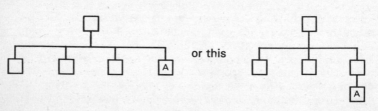

or this

Either way he has then got a clear line of authority — a manager who takes responsibility for him. There is someone to whom he can look when problems or priorities have to be sorted out, time allocations have to be agreed, standards of performance and behaviour have to be established, ideas about his future in the organisation have to be discussed.

**Crowd controller**: the boss whose job looks like X in this diagram:

He has too many subordinates for him to coordinate their work in any practical sense. With more than about ten people at most reporting to him, any manager can do little more than police individuals' efforts and supply on-the-spot problem-solving. Certainly he has little chance to integrate his group as a team. If he's at a senior level, even ten may be too many.

Possibly the diagram doesn't show this happening. X is supposed to be working through three or four direct subordinates who themselves are supposed to be 'managing' the others. But his constant by-passing is nevertheless making this the true picture. He is creating for himself a problem with his *span of control*. Through trying to direct everyone and everything — or simply being too available — he is overloading himself with self-created demands and wasting his effort in a mess of disorganised urgency. He leaves himself no time to think, no time to see where his priorities lie, no time to understand enough about what's going on so that he can take sensible decisions. And he cuts the ground from under the feet of his supposed direct subordinates. As managers, they are now useless to him.

So how many jobs should be directly accountable to one management position? There's no simple answer. It depends partly on the characteristics of the work, partly on the nature of people:

For the **work** the question is how difficult it is to coordinate the different responsibilities of the jobs. In many kinds of operation hardly any coordination is needed. Each person has his own workload which he can complete by himself without even considering what his colleagues are doing. There is simply no need for any interaction between the people involved. As far as the work is concerned, the only limit on the manager's effective span of control is the amount of supervision needed by each job and by the person doing it. It could be as many as fifteen or twenty people. Usually this is true only of certain kinds of work at the lowest levels in an organisation: jobs in a typing pool for instance, or simple repetitive manual work.

In other kinds of work, co-ordination between the different jobs is more necessary and harder to achieve. Imagine two researchers working to create the ultimate solvent, the stuff that will dissolve anything — *anything* at all. One is working in one laboratory on formulations for the solvent itself; the other is working in another laboratory trying to develop a container for the solvent. And the manager to whom they both report has his hands full trying to coordinate the work of just the pair of them.

Generally, the more complicated the effects of one job on another, the fewer subordinates a manager should have in his span of control. Even at a low level in the organisation a group of eight or nine interlocking jobs may be all that a supervisor or team leader can cope with. Fewer still if some work in different locations. At really high levels, the number may be as few as four or five.

> For the **people**, it's a question of how important it is for them to work as a team — either because of the needs of their work or simply to maintain their morale and commitment. Ten or eleven are probably the most that can truly feel themselves to be a team, pulling together as a single group. Over that number the group tends to fragment. Team-feeling is lost and cliques form inside the group. They can no longer act as a single well-integrated unit.

**One man and his dog**: the deputy problem when the job looks like this:

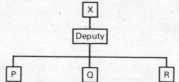

This is usually a nonsense. If it were true, it would mean that P, Q and R receive instructions only from the deputy and are accountable to him alone. X manages just one person — his deputy. If he starts giving any direct orders to the others or delegating to them, he is by-passing.

Perhaps this *is* sometimes so. The deputy is the real manager, with the nominal boss actually spending his time on DIY work or personal hobbies like 'long-term planning'. But otherwise, what *is* the deputy's job when X is there? Probably either a dumping-ground for odd activities no one else wants to be bothered with or the boss's gofer (gofer this and gofer that). So the job isn't any coherent piece of the action.

The point is that deputising for a boss isn't actually a separate job in terms of organisational structure. The deputy simply takes over the boss's job (or part of it) for the time being. Otherwise he has his own job to do:

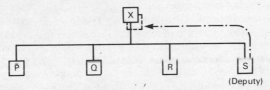

In any case, a one-to-one boss-subordinate arrangement is often a sign of poor organisation, particularly if they're both supposed to be managers. Spans of control can be too narrow — which may stem from the next form of rickets...

**Pecking order:** this is the structure with too many superior-subordinate levels. The diagram might look something like this:

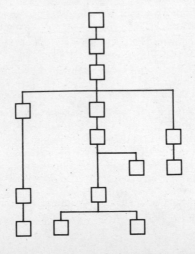

The level of each box on the paper is carefully calculated to represent the person's status or grade in the organisation. But if this truly represents the way the lines of authority and accountability work, it's likely to be a dog's breakfast of a structure. Look into what people actually do, and you'll probably find that no one is clear about what decisions are taken at which level. There's no particular system of allocating tasks other than by the kudos they offer, and the dog-work gets pushed down the line. What people *are* clear about is each individual's relative importance in the scheme of things: they're mistaking pecking order for organisation.

This raises the question of *levels of work*: how many levels should there be in an organisation structure? As a general rule, the fewer the better to keep the lines of formal communication and control short. But this has to be balanced against the need to avoid over-wide spans of control. Narrower spans, more levels; wider spans, fewer levels.

Some managers reckon that every extra level in a structure reduces the effectiveness of management control by twenty-five per cent. The figure may be a bit fanciful but the assessment is probably fair, even when all the managers involved are really capable. It's a gross underestimate if you compare these two structures:

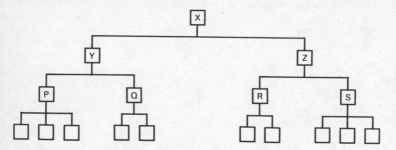

Four levels: Y and Z are senior long-service people for whom places have been created in the management hierarchy. Their main contribution is in fact their experience and ability in certain highly responsible specialist work. Giving them these management positions not only reduces the effectiveness of the whole management structure. It also diverts their time and energies from what they're really good at. It's even worse if they're each supposed to be responsible for their own specialism in the *other's* area.

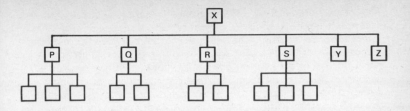

Three levels: X accepts that Y and Z have a contribution to make, but not fouling up his proper lines of formal communication. The two people concerned may well be higher-ranking than P, Q, R and S, but that's not what organisation structure is about.

Of course, only real levels count in this kind of exercise. You can't include mistakes in drawing the diagram — like management positions shown for deputies or assistants who aren't carrying a full managerial responsibility for the jobs shown below them. Nor can you include management jobs whose tenants are given no real management authority or are constantly being bypassed by their superiors. But those problems suggest even bigger inefficiencies going on, caused by the inevitable uncertainties over who's really responsible for what.

**Telephone exchange:** this problem isn't shown directly in a structure diagram — the job with too many lines of communication. It involves the person in it in too frequent a contact with too large a number of other people in the organisation for him to do the job efficiently. Most of the contacts are likely to be pieces of informal communication of course. Though the diagram doesn't represent these, it can be used as a starting point for spotting where the problem might exist.

Take a job in your area that you suspect might be overloaded with contacts, and count up the number of other jobs with which that person has a regular need for communication. Start with the formal lines, and then go on to all the informal communication links — essentially, whom he regularly talks with to pass information or requests or to discuss things that are relevant to his work or theirs. For the purpose of this exercise, links that consist of nothing but impersonal paperwork can generally be ignored (they don't pre-empt time in the same way, and usually don't demand the same understanding of the other person's role).

Many of the other jobs are likely to be off your diagram, in other parts of the organisation. If so, use another technique to chart the full range of communication links — drawing a *'Wheel of Contacts'*. Suppose you do this for your own job using the sort of pattern you see on the page opposite. The hub represents you. The spokes of the wheel represent all the lines of communication you're regularly involved in; the box at the end of each one says whom the contact is with. To make a better picture of what is actually happening, the length of the lines vary:

— shorter lines for the most frequent contacts: those you have daily, say, or several times a week.

— longer lines for the less frequent contacts: once or twice a week perhaps, or two or three times a month.

If a contact is much less frequent than this or happens only rarely or erratically, forget it. It's not likely to affect the day-to-day, week-to-week pressures of your job very much.

**The wheel of contacts**

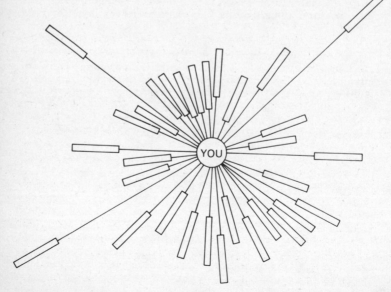

Once you've done this, what does it tell you about your job? If your Wheel of Contacts includes more than twenty-five to thirty lines or so, it might partly explain why you're always pressed for time, can never settle to one thing before another intrudes. Perhaps it's sometimes your own fault for being too available or failing to delegate. But the problem could point to a weakness in the organisational structure. If so, it will need a bit of deeper analysis to get to the bottom of it.

Take each of your contacts in turn and list the purposes it serves. What sort of information is passed? What kinds of question are discussed? Then look for the possibilities of reducing the number of different contacts:

- information you're now getting ad hoc from several sources — could you arrange for one person to provide it all for you? The same might apply with information you're giving to several people separately: you might be able to channel it through one or two of them to all the others.
- could you do more to share your load of contacts with your people? Perhaps you could give fuller responsibility to your subordinates for some of the communicating you're now doing yourself?
- could you reduce the frequency or unpredictability of some of your contacts — perhaps by making them into regular but more widely-spaced events.
- could a system you operate be simplified to reduce the number of people it involves you with?
- could you recommend some restructuring within the organisation to give you fewer, simpler or more systematic lines of communication?

Of course, it's always possible that the exercise reveals missing links in your wheel of contacts — people or units in the organisation that you don't communicate with but who ought to be there. Sorting out your lines of communication may make it possible to create necessary new links without overloading yourself.

The communication problem in most organisations isn't lack of information. There's usually too much of the stuff churning around the system. It's a problem of getting the right information to the right point at the right time — which depends on whether the structure has the right points to get it to and well-designed routes for getting it there. It's not unknown for a boss who's trying to cope with umpteen lines of communication to be sitting on a piece of information that his subordinates urgently need for their work. They don't know he has it. He doesn't realise its relevance for them. But that's part of the next problem.

**Send three and fourpence:** this is the old joke aobut the military communication over a long and unreliable telephone connection. What started as "send reinforcements, we're going to advance" arrived as "send three and fourpence, we're going to a dance". If communication lines are to long, information gets distorted or lost. The more people involved in getting messages from A to B, the more likely it is that B gets an incomplete and even wrong idea of what A said.

The problem is caused by managers who don't understand the difference between formal and informal communication. They insist on everything going through them. Of course they need to be kept in the picture. But there are better ways of doing that than to have each manager turn himself into an essential link in the lengthening chain of people involved in getting each message through. Often all they achieve is to complicate it, give it the wrong emphasis, or stifle its point under a load of political padding.

Do you try to stop your people discussing their work directly with others who are involved but outside your area of control? Do you make a practice of editing their every memo or report before it goes out to its intended readers? Do you deny your subordinates the opportunity to attend meetings relevant to their work simply because you feel their status doesn't entitle them to be there? Do you sometimes delay some information getting past you on the grounds that it isn't precisely correct, when the speed it reaches its destination is more important than its details? Then you've no right to complain of a communication problem. You are part of it.

**Hell:** the hot spot occupied by managers who are given responsibilities but without the corresponding authority. They're expected to achieve targets imposed by their bosses, but haven't the right to object if the workloads are impossible to accomplish. They're required to get the work done to set standards, but have to accept whoever Personnel assigns to vacancies in their areas, suitable or otherwise. They're supposed to maintain high productivity, but have no effective sanctions for slackers among their staffs.

A lot of foremen and supervisors are in this situation. Senior people often express a naïve view of them as 'the end of the executive chain' — there to organise and control shop floor work, to convert the policies of higher management into action, to feed information upwards for decision-making, to de-fuse potential industrial relations problems in cooperation with the shop steward. Most of this is clap-trap. A report on a wide-ranging investigation a few years ago presented a more realistic view. Most foremen cannot sack or even suspend employees however grave the offence. They are allowed no part in decisions to engage or promote. They cannot authorise overtime, even within the narrowest limits. They are rarely consulted over decisions on the jobs or work in their areas. They are regularly bypassed by their bosses.

Not that a structure diagram will reveal this, but job descriptions of the type we've discussed might show where the problem exists. It will be damned difficult to explain how the responsibilities can be fulfilled within the boundaries that actually exist. Possibly that might stimulate some thought about reconstructing the supervisory role to accept the facts of life· the shop floor themselves do much of the planning and control of their own work. Power is already being shared. The question is whether the sharing is being done effectively.

In many cases it makes more sense to accept that the supervisor's job has been reduced to just three main responsibilities:

1. Coping with the unexpected: overcoming interruptions to the work flow, sorting out bunching of the work, plugging holes in the system, getting things made by Friday...

2. Deciding when specialists need to be called in: keeping an eye open for equipment malfunctions, jobs that turn out to need expert treatment, things that need attention if they're not to cause trouble.

3. Maintaining his own relationship with the workforce: passing on information from upstairs, watching discipline and performance, listening for squeaks and rattles, exercising leadership as far as his capabilities and the situation will allow — and reporting problems back up to whoever *has* got the authority to deal with them.

... to which one further responsibility might be added. It's not one the supervisor is often encouraged or even expected to get involved in, but he's usually better-placed than anyone else to take it on:

4. Undertaking projects to improve work methods and

systems in his area: investigating problems with workflow and backlogs, seeking to simplify or strengthen planning and control procedures, looking for ways in which economies could be made in materials, equipment, time or effort — collecting information and formulating ideas on policy or system changes for more senior decisions.

**Flying Elephant:** the organisation structure that's unsuited to its purpose. It separates activities that should be combined; it hampers cooperation to get things done; it causes waste of time and effort. Worst of all, it demoralises people. Possibly it was designed by an amateur taxidermist — or simply growed like Topsy — and no one has since had the nous or nerve to try restructuring it's anatomy.

In an organisation, responsibilities can be allocated in different ways between different divisions, different departments, different branches or sections. Even a supervisor has some scope for ideas about the way the total work on his patch is divided between the various jobs his people do. If he can see a better method of arranging it, he might himself have the freedom to put it into practice. At the very least he should have the responsibility to suggest it to his boss. But it does require some understanding of what's involved in dividing work between different jobs or units (i.e. groups of jobs) in an organisation structure. That's our next point.

# D. Division of work

There are many different possibilities for organisation structures. Each of them uses a different *principle of division* for splitting up the work between the various units in the structure. The ability to think out the best way of doing this division is one of the skills of logical thinking we dealt with in our first book in this series, *What is a Manager?* There we called it the skill of **sectioning**.

One aspect of this skill is the ability to take a collection of things — operations and activities in this case — and to find a method of dividing them into sections that relate to each other in a consistent way. To quote the explanation we gave:

''The system uses one, and only one, principle of division

to separate its sections one from another. For instance, the jobs of a number of salesmen might be divided by the geographical areas they cover *or* the types of customers they call on *or* the products they sell. But in a logical system you can't have some jobs defined by the areas covered, some by the customers visited and some by the products sold. If you do have a mess like this, be prepared for all sorts of problems of co-ordination".

Of course, the structure of a big organisation may use many principles of division at the different levels of management. Its major groups may be divided by one principle, the departments within a group by another principle, the sections within a department by yet a third and so on — right down to the way the individual jobs are separated within a single team on the shop floor or in an office. There's nothing wrong in that. It's the way it has to be. The question for each manager at each level is this: "Have I got the best way of separating the area I control into units?" It's a question he can resolve by looking at three things: the purpose of his whole operation, the co-ordination that's required inside it, and the co-ordination that's needed with other areas of the organisation. If the answer he finds satisfies all three conditions, his area is probably well-structured.

That doesn't mean he has no further problems. Every scheme of dividing work has its strengths and weaknesses, and it's important for managers to recognise what they are. They can then be on their guard to ensure the problems are kept under reasonable control.

These are some of the more common principles that organisational structures actually use, and the problems their managers should be aware of and try to counter:

**Line/staff**: division by the way the work relates to the end-result the organisation is there to achieve. 'Line' is any activity that is essential to that end-result: in a manufacturing company, for example, it's the work that starts with buying raw materials or whatever, and ends with products that the customers have paid for. 'Staff' are all the jobs that act as services to the Line: such functions as Management Accounting, Personnel, Industrial Relations and the various administrative operations. Often they are grouped together as head office functions, but that's not the only possibility. The real point of the Line/Staff split is that it enables Staff units to provide their services across the whole range of Line functions.

Problems arise when Staff try to take over the proper authority of the Line managers. But it's at least equally likely that managers in the Line try to abdicate their responsibilities to Staff. Production managers claim that poor morale on the shop floor isn't their problem to deal with — it's for the people in Industrial Relations to sort out. Administrative managers complain about the clerical recruits that Personnel has selected, but don't want to be involved themselves in the recruitment. Managers of all types and descriptions are happy to assume that Training has the full responsibility for their subordinates' development of knowledge and ability (or the lack of it). And people everywhere seem to think that the Finance Department has the financial performance of every other part of the organisation firmly under its own control. Even the financial boys themselves can get to believe it.

Not so. All of these things are the responsibility of Line managers, from the chief executive down to the supervisors. The Staff functions are there to help them fulfil it, not to try to handle it all on their own account. In practice that's impossible. The attempt results in all kinds of crossed wires and things left undone because someone thought someone else was looking after it. Line managers are there to *manage*.

**Process**: division by the different process stages in any operation from its input to its output. For an organisation as a whole, this is the commonest method of dividing up the work of the Line into departments: research and development, purchasing, stores, production, distribution, sales, customer accounts. Some of these major units are similarly sub-divided — production for instance into the different manufacturing processes through which all the products go. Even people's individual jobs on the shop floor or in the office can be arranged as consecutive stages in whatever is being done there: every person is restricted to one specified operation on each piece of work that goes through. The whole arrangement depends on how effectively each unit plays its part.

This puts process division perpetually at the mercy of the co-ordination between its units. There's a major problem when they get isolated from each other. Sometimes this seems a deliberate intention of managers in each department — they indulge in a game of point-scoring against their supposed colleagues in other departments. More often it stems from simple lack of interest in the other units' operations and problems.

Either way, the whole system then serves to frustrate those in the later stages when they suffer from things going wrong somewhere back up the line. Just possibly, a manager running that earlier process stage might realise the difficulty his operation is creating for the *next* stage. But he'll often fail to see the chain of cause-and-effect much further than that. With process division, the communication links need to be fast and efficient right along the whole line.

There is often another problem when process division is carried right down to the workforce level: it can result in very repetitive and boring jobs. One answer might be to develop a method of job rotation for the people involved. Another might be to involve them more in developing the coordination that's needed. Yet another more complete solution is often possible — to change the structure into a 'product' division.

**Product**: division by the different things made or the different services provided to the 'market' (which might be the users of an end-result *inside* the organisation). This has the advantage of creating units that are more independent than with process division. Each one is self-contained: within it are all the processes it requires for creating the product or service it supplies. On the grand scale it is the way a company like ICI organises itself — into major divisions that act to a large extent as separate manufacturing organisations. On the small scale it can operate on the shop floor: Volvo's system of teams for car assembly work for instance — each small group of workers organises its own working arrangements to build complete cars one at a time. In product division, the function of the different units are defined by the *end-results* each one produces rather than by the *operations* they each perform.

But there can still be problems with product division. Certainly it can give people more pride in the results they achieve, more commitment to the units in which they work. But the different units don't depend on each other in the way they are forced to willy-nilly by process division and so communication between them can vanish. Efforts may be duplicated: what one unit produces may overlap with another's output, or different units may each spend considerable time overcoming the same kind of problem. Their demands on other, differently-structured areas may not be co-ordinated. Their people with specialist skills may not be able to use them effectively for the area as a whole.

To overcome these problems doesn't usually require the

117

speed and efficiency of communication that's needed between process units. It's more a question of keeping the units in mind of the fact they're all rowing the same boat — perhaps a system of regular meetings between their managers or supervisors to share knowledge, problems and ideas and to work out their methods of joint liaison with other areas in the organisation.

**Market:** division by the kinds of customer served (whether real ones, or users of a service inside the organisation). It's the basis of many a sales or service organisation — for instance, a builders merchant's trade and DIY operations or a newspaper's editorial and advertisement departments. Many a sales department is split up the same way, the different sales units each selling to one type of customer in the company's total market. It has the great merit of focusing the attention of people in each unit on the needs of customers in just one part of the total market. This enables them to become expert in selling to that particular type of customer — or in serving their needs if the 'customers' are in fact people in other parts of the organisation itself.

But such a structure can create uncoordinated pressures on other, differently-structured departments — on Purchasing or Production for example. And if the customer categories overlap or their interests conflict, guerilla warfare can break out between the units. It's usually essential to have efficient systems for regulating the demands on other departments. There's also a need for good management of the boundaries between the different units' responsibilities — including rapid information to managers upstairs whenever a clash is threatened.

**Geographic:** division by the locations in which the work is done or by the territories served. Another common principle of division in sales or service organisation. The regions allocated to sales teams in a sales force is an example, or the branch organisation of a bank, or the way in which chains of shops or hotels are structured. Each unit's work is defined by the area in which it operates. For many organisations there is no alternative.

Even when there's a choice, the advantages of this kind of structure make it very attractive. Each unit's managers and their people can identify with their area and get a sense of independence and pride in their 'ownership' of it. They get to know its characteristics and possibilities, and can use that knowledge to make their operations more effective. Geographic division can also economise in each unit's costs of distributing its products and in the travel time and expenses of its staff.

But there is a reverse side to the coin. The units often lack a sense of common interest. Poor communication between them is a frequent weakness, and sometimes causes severe disadvantages for the organisation as a whole. Customers moving from one unit's area to another's can be put off by the variations in the standard of service they get. Their business may be permanently lost as a result. And it is often difficult if not impossible to arrange transfers of people between the units for experience or promotion: if it's done, valuable members of staff may begin to resent the effects on themselves and their families of regular uprootings.

Well-defined policies and standards are needed for the various units' performance, and efficient systems of control. These things are often difficult to get right because of the way the territories and resources of the units vary. Policies have to be skilfully conceived to allow for the different possibilities and constraints of the different areas. There has to be enough freedom for each unit manager, given the conditions in his area, to make the best use of his resources and to exploit the opportunities that emerge in his patch.

**Know-how**: division by the different kinds of expertise involved. The people in each unit all share a single discipline. They have similar knowledge and skills. This is very much like process division, where each unit usually needs one kind of ability to handle the work done at that stage. But in division by know-how, the operations don't follow one another in a series of stages. The work of each unit is governed simply by the abilities of its people, not by the needs of other units down the line.

In fact this is quite a common principle of division. It's seen more often in the Staff departments that provide different kinds of expertise to the Line: personnel, training, industrial relations, work study, organisation and methods, management accounting, internal auditing, marketing services and so on. It's also the basis of the division that local government makes between its professional groups and the administrative teams who support them (which isn't really a Line/Staff split — the work of the admin officers is often an important element in the end-results a local authority produces). It's even used to allocate work between individual people: Fred gets these tasks because they're what he's good at; Mary gets those because she's better at them.

There are advantages in putting together people working in the same field. Since they share a common interest, it

119

encourages them to work together to develop their expertise and their methods of using it to the organisation's benefit. Standards are easier to maintain. Policies are easier to define.

The problems stem mainly from the attitudes encouraged by know-how division. The different units may lack the interest or incentive to explore the ways in which other groups' abilities and experience could be coupled with their own expertise. It is easy for the people in each discipline to become obsessive about it. They can come to regard anyone outside it with contempt — even those it is their job to collaborate with. Empire-building is often rife.

If you are a manager at the receiving end of these problems, it's hard to know how to react. Do you accept that the experts must be right and bow to their superior wisdom? Or do you insist they serve what *you* see as your needs, give them a clear specification of what you want — and then, if their advice doesn't suit you, reject it? In the first case you may find they are solving their own problems rather than yours. In the second you're like a patient telling your doctor what medical treatment to give you: you get minimal value from their expertise.

There is a third alternative: to get enough understanding of what their discipline can offer you so that you can work *with* them in defining needs and arriving at solutions. That way you get results that are both sound in theory and workable in practice.

And for those inside the knowhow-divided units? There is sometimes the opportunity to extend their horizons by getting them involved in inter-disciplinary projects...

**Project**: division by the different projects or programmes that have to be completed. It shares many of the characteristics of product division but with one key difference: each unit has a *single* end-result to achieve — a new product in production or a building completed or a system in operation or a problem solved. Think of ship builders, construction companies, civil engineers, management consultants, research and development organisations. The work of all of them consists of large-scale projects — one after another, running concurrently, overlapping each other. Then think of working parties formed to plan a scheme, to reorganise a department, to create a new method of doing something. Each one is an example of project organisation. The people are brought together at the start and a project manager is appointed; when the project is completed they disperse — perhaps to re-form into further teams for new projects.

120

A project team contains all the abilities needed for its tasks; often that means that it has to blend together people from different disciplines. But in many a large-scale project, the nature of the tasks change from stage to stage. As the tasks change, some people leave and others join because the different tasks require different abilities. When the whole project is complete, the jobs of all the project staff are at an end.

So project division sets a premium on the organisation's efficiency in deploying its manpower. It also puts a premium on managers' ability to create good teamwork among people who may not have worked together before. That takes time, and time is what you haven't got when a project is under way.

The small-scale project done by a working party is a different matter. The group is usually a small one and its membership fairly stable. As often as not, the project is a part-time exercise for all concerned — they still have their regular work to attend to. For the project leader, the exercise can serve as a useful introduction to the responsibilities of management.

Whatever the size of the project, it demands some ability in planning. A large project may contain dozens of interlocking tasks, and this often calls for quite sophisticated techniques of scheduling peoples' activities to try to prevent one thing from delaying another. Later we'll look at the kinds of techniques that can be used. But even a small project needs thinking through in advance — which is a skill many managers and supervisors don't seem to find much need for in their day-to-day work. To tackle the occasional problem-solving or work-improvement project with your colleagues or subordinates may give some useful practice to develop that skill, quite apart from the value of the result you achieve.

**Workload**: an arbitrary division of people into groups, each capable of handling a roughly similar workload. It's done mainly for administrative convenience — or sometimes you might cynically suspect to produce a neat and tidy-looking structure diagram.

It's frequently seen in clerical and administrative functions, particularly those of large public bodies. For instance, a department of clerical officers may be processing forms sent in by members of the public. It is divided into three sections: the first deals with members of the public whose names begin with the letters A–F, the second with letters G–N, the third with letters O–Z. Another department may handle a case-load of applications for approvals of some kind, and is organised similarly into sections. New cases are allocated between the sections simply on the basis of which section has the smallest backlog of outstanding cases.

They're both workload division. The only difference is that the first department has decided the allocations in advance, the second decides them on the spot. This is just like the "who's free?" method of allocating work between the different people within a section — that's the same principle applied to individual jobs.

The one thing you can say for this way of dividing work is that it's an easy one to operate. Unless it's really badly supervised, there's no difficulty in keeping people busy — if that's the object of the exercise. The real question is whether the manager who structures his units this way couldn't have found a more purposeful system of division.

The trouble is that workload division gives people minimal responsibility, so it can't do much to engage their interest or commitment. Each of the other methods of dividing work creates a purpose for each unit that lies beyond the simple performance of task after task after task after task...

- process division gets it playing a part towards a bigger end-result.
- product division creates a sense of team pride in what's produced.
- market division builds an involvement with the customer or user of the output.

... and so on. But workload division simply gives the people in each unit things to do. Unless their managers use a bit of imagination in setting up targets and standards and in trying to involve them in making the allocations, there is no consistent goal for people to work towards as individuals or as teams.

Now look back at your structure diagram. Can you recognise the principles by which it divides the work at each level? Could any level be structured differently to give you or your people a clearer sense of purpose or to make things easier to coordinate and control? If so, what can you do about it as a manager?

The answer depends largely on the next aspect of organising — the rules defined in policy statements and the scope they allow you for tackling organisational problems yourself. But even where you're restricted by the policies of your superiors, you've got a responsibility to point out the problems and the inefficiencies they cause on your own patch. It's better still if you can suggest the kinds of change your boss could implement to cure them.

# E. Policy statements

On a clear December night in 1982 two North Sea ferries approached each other on opposite courses just off the English coast. To avoid a collision, both altered course — and steered straight into each other. A large hole was ripped in the side of one and she rapidly filled with water and went down. Six people were drowned. But for the fact that all this happened in shallow water, the loss of life could have been enormous.

At the public enquiry that followed, the collision raised many questions about the two captain's judgement and about the decisions they'd made within the rules of maritime law. But the focal point became the sinking itself. There is a regulation governing the watertight doors of a ship at sea which requires them to be closed except when 'necessarily open for the working of the ship'. If the doors in the holed vessel had been closed she would have remained afloat — but they weren't. Was her captain in breach of the regulation, or was the regulation itself not well enough specified or enforced? The enquiry officials found it a difficult question to answer.

Regulations and laws are rules made by governments and their agencies. Policies are rules made by managements. It's essential to have them in each case. Without laws, a country would have no effective way of ordering its citizens' behaviour towards each other and towards the institutions that maintain their way of life. Without policies an organisation would become a disorganised mess, its managers lacking any means to direct and harmonise their people's activities or their own. But like official regulations, the policies need to be clear, unambiguous and properly enforced. Often they're not. Then, like the enquiry officials, managers are faced with a problem.

Suppose one of your subordinates has done something that has gone disastrously wrong. Was it simply poor judgement, or was a rule broken? The difference is important. If no rule existed, you can't criticise him for using his judgement however severely you criticise the way he used it. If a clear rule was knowingly flouted, he didn't have the right to use his judgement however sensible it may have seemed to him at the time. It's a disciplinary offence. But what if the rule is uncertain? Then no one knows where they stand, and you're in a dilemma over how to deal with the problem. Treat it as an error of judgement, and you may be at fault in weakening an important area of your organisation's policy. Discipline your subordinate and you can stand accused of acting unreasonably and unfairly. If there's a rule, there should be no doubt about it in anyone's mind.

The point is that managers have just two options for controlling their people's work. In each aspect of the work it has to be quite clear which option they are taking. One is to control things in arrears: you decide on the spot what is and isn't acceptable — which means you don't step in until something has already happened that you're dissatisfied with. The other is to control things in advance: before the action begins, people know the rules on what they must do and mustn't do.

There's a skill in making the choice. If a policy is established for something where the question of right or wrong depends very much on circumstances at the time, it will produce some idiotic results. Those people who prefer to duck responsibility and to 'go by the book' will make it an excuse for not using their judgement when it's essential to do so. Others who see the rule's idiocy will become all the more convinced that rules are generally stupid and will be further encouraged to break them whenever they think they can get away with it. Then no one knows where they are.

But if the point is important and circumstances only rarely come into the picture, it's a different matter. Then there should be a policy. If one *isn't* established on something where a principle is at stake or where the managers concerned can be perfectly clear about what's needed, that creates disrespect for their management. Worse, it means their organisation doesn't work effectively at that point. They're constantly reduced to controlling their people by a sort of 'find out what little Tommy is up to and stop him'! If there's no rule, Tommy can reasonably feel they don't know what *they're* up to. With a sensible rule that Tommy knows, there's at least an even chance he'll stop himself. And if he doesn't, he can't feel hard done by when he's disciplined for it. Indeed, he ought to expect it.

As a manager you depend on policy to define your own freedom of action. True it creates limits to your freedom, but by doing the same for everyone else — your colleagues, superiors, subordinates and others — it also protects your authority to use that freedom. The clearer the rules are, the more certainty you have about your right to exercise your authority. But the policies themselves have to be properly constructed in the first place, which means finding good answers to five different questions:
- do policies exist where they're needed?
- do people know what are and aren't matters of policy?
- is each policy clearly understood by everyone it applies to?
- is each policy properly enforced?
- are policies kept-up-to-date?

Let's take each one of them in turn to see what's involved:

# Do policies exist where they're needed?

If something important *could* be regulated by a rule but isn't, there ought to be a good reason why not. Perhaps you can argue that it would be less effectively done that way — and often you might be right, all things considered. But otherwise there are many, many things that need clear policies on the way they're handled to prevent uncertainty, disputes and general sloppiness.

In the list that follows, you'll find most of the issues on which organisations commonly have policies. Use it to identify any specific points you're not sure about in the policies of your own organisation — or of your department or section within it: questions you should ask your boss — "do we have a policy on this?"; questions you should ask yourself — "should I establish a rule for my people on that?"

**The work:**
- the major operational systems of the organisation that affect your area: those that control the work it takes on, purchasing and stocks, production programming, work-flow and work-in-progess, sales administration etc.
- the particular methods and techniques used in your area.
- professional or departmental codes of practice.
- workloads and performance standards.
- time allowances and deadlines.
- manning levels and work allocations.
- equipment and plant utilisation.

How do your superiors' policies restrict your freedom to decide your own policies on your people's work? Do you *have* clear rules on what's expected of your people — the amount of work they're expected to do and its quality? What authority do you have to act if it's not done?

**Levels of authority:**
- the sources of authority for making policies and rules.
- the authority allocated to jobs at each level of management for day-to-day decisions.
- the lines of authority and accountability (i.e. formal communication).
- restrictions on what can be delegated.

In the area you command, what can and what can't you change?

For changes you haven't the authority to make, how far above you is the person who does have the authority?

## Job boundaries:
- division of responsibility between your area and others for activities that you're both involved in.
- information channels between you (i.e. informal communication).
- authority of specialists who provide services to your area.
- your authority and rights of appeal over decisions taken by others that have effects in your area.

What aspects of these things are defined by policies? Which are left to be worked out between you?

## Legal requirements:
- health and safety legislation.
- employment legislation.
- commercial law.
- transport and traffic regulations etc. etc.

Which of these can affect the operations you manage? What policies exist to ensure compliance with the law? What further policies does the organisation have on these matters as a matter of good business practice, social responsibility etc? What constraints do they put on your own decision-making?

## Personal policies:
- terms and conditions of employment.
- recruitment and selection policies.
- induction procedures.
- job placements and transfers.
- promotions and regrading.
- training and development.
- retirements, redundancies and dismissals.

What aspects of each of these are regulated by policies for the organisation generally? Which are matters of departmental policy? What responsibilities and authority do Personnel and Training functions have in your area? How does that chime in with your own responsibilities and authority over your people?

## Pay policies:
- pay scales and the rules governing them.
- grading by responsibility and work.

- overtime payments.
- pay during sickness and other absences.
- bonuses and extra payments.

How do policies on these matters restrict your freedom in allocating work? What have you the authority to decide?

## Attendance and timekeeping:
- hours of work and policies on mealtimes and other breaks.
- overtime working.
- shiftwork.
- absences from work.
- holiday entitlements.

How are the rules defined? What is and isn't a matter of policy — where can you make your own special arrangements with your people? Where do you have to seek higher approval?

## The disciplinary code:
- the range of situations covered by rules of discipline.
- the kinds of personal behaviour prohibited by the rules.
- management authority over infringements and misconduct.
- disciplinary procedures and how they're invoked.
- protection of employees' rights.
- appeal procedures.
- handling complaints and grievances.

You *must* know what policy is on all these things — and there should *be* policies. Otherwise you're at a disadvantage against an astute 'barrack-room lawyer'.

### Industrial relations:
- how relationships between managers and union or staff representatives are codified.
- what are accepted as the proper concerns of representatives.
- issues that can be negotiated at each management level.
- the limits to what commitments can be entered into.

If there are Industrial Relations staff in the organisation, how are responsibilities and authority divided between you and them?

What can they insist on, and what have you the right to treat simply as advice?

**Dealings with outsiders:**
- restrictions on the negotiation of arrangements or deals with customers, suppliers, contractors etc.
- purchasing or sales terms and conditions, procedures etc.
- rules on the disclosure of information to anyone outside.
- conduct prejudicial to the organisation's interests or repute.
- rules on giving or receiving gifts, tips etc.

**Personal arrangements and expenses:**
- expenses allowable and how they're claimed.
- travel arrangements, car allowances etc.
- meals and accommodation.
- entertaining and out-of-pocket expenses.
- cash advances and other forms of personal assistance.

**Security of cash:**
- handling and accounting for cash transactions.
- movements and safe-keeping of cash.
- petty cash controls.
- making or receiving payments by cheque, credit card etc.

**Management of physical resources and property:**
- procedures for stock receipts and issues.
- control and requisitioning of stock.
- dealing with redundant stock.
- protection of attractive goods.
- action on losses or 'shrinkage'.
- protection of information and information systems.
- prevention of damage to equipment and plant — rules on its operation and maintenance.
- protection of buildings against hazards of fire, unauthorised entry etc.
- rules on outsiders entering the organisation's premises.

**Financial controls:**
- budgeting procedures budgetary allocations.

- budgetary controls and the treatment of variances above or below budget.
- costing methods and rules on cost allocations.
- purchasing and sales acounting systems.
- pricing policies and credit control.
- auditing requirements.

There are bound to be many, many policies regulating such things as these. Where your area is involved, do you know what the rules are? What authority do the management accountants have for decisions that affect things you're responsible for? What have you the authority to negotiate with them? Where can they only advise you?

On many of these issues, the same policies must apply throughout the whole organisation (i.e. policies authorised by its top management for their total area of command). Further policies will apply in your department that don't apply to others (policies defined by your department head for *his* area of command). Yet more policies will exist for different divisions within the department — down to the specific policies that *you* have established for your own area.

If you're a supervisor, don't think you've nothing to do with policy-making yourself. Think of it as making rules — that is what policies are. If you're any sort of manager, you're bound to be operating some things fairly strictly that *you* see as important. The question is whether you realise what rules you have thereby created for your people's activities and behaviour. Your methods of management may be too lax, or they may be too restrictive — in ways you've never actually considered. But whether you've declared the constraints or not, they still exist.

When you do decide to institute a new or revised policy, be sure of your ground: have you the authority to make it? Is it really needed? Have you got its details right? Remember you're issuing a standing instruction that's got some permanence about it. Both you and those it applies to are going to have to live with it, so it needs more careful consideration than your ordinary run of day-to-day decisions.

One occasion when you *don't* create a rule is when you're in the middle of a difficult situation caused (as you might see it) by the lack of one. Don't be pushed into it by anyone else's insistence or your own short temper. Instant policy is nearly always bad policy. You need time to think through the implications so that once you declare it you don't have to amend it the following week — or worse still, try to pretend you didn't mean it. That raises doubts about whether you mean what you say in other matters. It reduces your personal credibility.

Now the second of the five questions that need answering (remember?):

## 2. Do people know what are and aren't matters of policy?

Policy isn't just the do's and don'ts that managers officially require their people to obey. Policy is also what their people unofficially believe is required or sanctioned. If they don't realise that something they're doing is breaking the rules, the official policy can hardly be said to be the real one. It's a fiction until they're told about it — or reprimanded for infringing it (which is hardly the best way for them to learn that the rule exists).

It works the other way round too. If people persist with something out of a widespread but mistaken idea that it's policy, that makes it policy to all intents and purposes. And it remains so until they're specifically told it's not.

Policies get established in different ways. Anyone who thinks it's done solely by managers deciding they'll have a rule on this or that is being naïve. People guess policy by noticing what their superiors seem to expect, by interpreting their bosses' comments and criticisms, by being allowed to continue with customs and practices that are perhaps ineffective or inappropriate without anyone in authority questioning them. Even a casual remark from someone above them on a particular case can become a 'policy' that's rigidly applied to anything they consider similar. Their managers may not realise what's happening.

You'll find lots of odd beliefs in organisations about what does and doesn't constitute policy:

    — people imagine it's 'policy' to write anything in a formal and unreadable style. So do their managers often enough: they'll criticise an informal letter or memo on the grounds that the managers above *them* would object. But you'll rarely find anyone up there who'll admit to authorship of such a policy.

    — supervisors suppose it isn't their place to make any rules at all about what they expect of their work-people. They accept they're just there to deal with the emergencies and crises caused by the lack of discipline or of proper work standards below them. Their superiors often have no policies whatsoever on the question either, don't even realise the problem exists if their own supervision is poor.

— managers sometimes assume that policy forbids any communication outside the formal lines of authority. They try to stop their people from discussing work matters with anyone beyond their own command — even with others who are directly affected or involved. When they're asked who instituted such a ridiculous rule, they claim that the structure diagrams their superiors have drawn up for their areas require it. This is usually news to the superiors.

True, policy is often just being used as an excuse in such cases. But they underline the importance of making clear what *isn't* official policy as well as what is.

Sometimes a policy may even be required *not* to have unofficial policies on a certain point — which may mean disciplining managers who still try to operate unnecessary and inefficient rules on the point. It has been done. In a big engineering company, staff throughout one major function were being trained in a simple, direct style of letter and report writing. When they returned from the courses, many of their managers ruled that they must continue to use the old formal style. The director who had authorised the training eventually had to issue a directive prohibiting this policy. Staff were to be left free to use whatever style they judged was most effective.

### 3. Is each policy clearly understood by everyone it applies to?

A policy is a reasonably permanent kind of rule. With time, people's ideas about it can develop all sorts of variations that simply aren't valid. Some may even forget it, which means the rule won't be applied consistently. After all, it's only one out of perhaps hundreds of policies that exist in the organisation, and they can't all be remembered. To try to maintain the entire body of policy by relying on people's capacities to hold it all in mind is something of a forlorn hope. Yet it's a hope that many organisations seem happy to rely on.

This can cause endless disputes over exactly how the policy on this or that was originally defined. It also gives ample scope for excuses when a rule has been broken. These things weaken managers' authority and control throughout the organisation.

There's no other way around it: policies have to be drawn together and **written down** — all of them, official and unofficial. This may require investigations to find out those traditionally established but previously unwritten rules that are actually being maintained in spite of official policy. It forces managers to recognise the hidden codes and practices that pervade their organisations and to make decision about them: should they be allowed to persist? Many of them may in fact be more effective than official policy itself. In any case, if they're accepted they become part of official policy and can be seen for what they really are. If not, the fact can be publicly declared so that no one need be in doubt about it.

The process begins with top management issuing statements of the policies they decide or authorise for the whole organisation (many of which may actually be drafted by specialists in functions like Finance, Personnel, Industrial Relations, Engineering and so on). Managers at each level below them issue further policy statements as additions to those of top management for their own departments or functions.

By the time this process reaches your level, most of the ground rules should have been established. You have to think only of the particular rules required for your area's work. But remember you're responsible for seeing that everyone below you understands *all* the policies relevant to them — yours *and* those established upstairs. That is far easier to do if they've been assembled in a form that's readily available for refrence.

Make no mistake about it, all this involves a hell of a lot of time and work. Many managers who prefer seat-of-the-pants management and instant decision-making will be disinclined to make the effort. But have they considered the net saving they'd get if they replaced their disorganised and improvised methods of leadership wih clear and consistent rules?

The chairman of a large organisation once described just such an exercise in his company. Managers and union representatives met to draw up a series of policy statements or 'standing orders' as he called them. They created rules for the whole company on many of the issues of personnel, pay, attendance, discipline, industrial relations etc. that we listed a few pages back:

> "each order involved twenty or thirty people in many hours of work. But over the years, those standing orders have saved us tens of thousands of hours, eliminated countless disputes, and given properly delineated freedom of action to hundreds of managers. They have enabled the managers to make decisions that are backed by clear authority agreed to by all parties. When circumstances changed, the orders were revised

relatively easily because everyone could appreciate the fact that they had become outmoded''.

## 4. Is each policy properly enforced?

If a rule isn't consistently applied it creates uncertainty and injustice. Discipline one person for failing to conform, and he can reasonably feel he has been harshly treated if he can point to others getting away with it. It also makes the manager who *is* trying to be consistent unsure of himself when he's dealing with infringements: can he be firm if he feels he is thereby being unfair? Besides that, a nasty feeling can develop that managers are choosing to enforce whichever of their superiors' policies suit their own convenience or their personal fads.

And that isn't all that's at stake. Rule-breaking has a snowball effect. Let a few people do it, and soon the majority who otherwise would be perfectly willing to conform will be ignoring the rule too. If just a few office staff begin regularly to pack up ten minutes before the end of working hours, before long precious little work will be done by *anyone* in that office during those ten minutes. Then you've got a problem to recover the situation: a rule that has been allowed to lapse is often far harder to reimpose than it is to create a new rule altogether.

If a policy is stated, presumably there is a need for it. And if so, then repeated failure to observe it is damaging to the organisation in some way. So what might cause a problem with its enforcement?

— **the policy is a poor one.** Perhaps it seems unnecessary. Perhaps it doesn't make enough allowance for exceptions to the rule. Perhaps it's simply unworkable: the situations to which it applies simply can't be handled in the way the policy supposes they can.

For instance, suppose you have a policy for how much work your people should do in a specified time. Many managers try to set the rules simply by guessing how long it takes to do each task or by relying on paperwork records — and set standards that are either impossibly high or ridiculously low. Somehow you've got to establish what's a reasonable working speed to demand, even if you've got to do the task yourself to find out

— **the policy is poorly defined.** It isn't specific enough, or it's worded in a complicated way. If some people don't understand it, how can anyone hope to enforce it consistently?

A policy statement is the equivalent of a law or official regulation, but that doesn't mean it's to be written in a kind of legalese. It should be simple and clear enough to allow no one the excuse that he misunderstood it. It should give all the information anyone might need about the policies it contains:
— what precisely is each policy and what does it apply to? Is it clear what it requires or forbids?
— who does it apply to and in what circumstances?
— on whose authority was the statement issued and on what date?
— how can exceptions be made — who can authorise them?

**The policy was introduced in the wrong way.** In large organisations, many of the general rules that apply to their employees and workpeople are worked out in collaboration with union or staff representatives. That way they're more likely to be accepted by everyone, and enforcing them is less of a problem. Yet a manager who wants to institute a policy for other managers subordinate to him will often do it without involving them in any way. It's presented to them as an edict. The result is often a policy which is both a poor one because it doesn't take account of facts they would have pointed out, and one they resent because of the way it was introduced. The policy seems unreasonable to them, and may actually *be* unreasonable.

Even when you can be quite clear about the basic rule that you're going to establish, there's usually something to be gained from discussing the way it's defined with those to whom it will apply. Once they realise there's going to be a policy come what may, their involvement in framing it can persuade them to accept the fact. They can often help you make the policy more workable too — pointing out problems it must allow for and suggesting how you can overcome the next problem...

**The policy has no effective controls.** Managers cannot enforce a policy if they don't know whether or not it's being infringed. It has to be possible for them to check that their subordinates are observing the policy and, if the subordinates are also managers, that they are maintaining it in *their* areas of command.

With many kinds of policy, control is simply a matter of keeping in touch with what is going on — physically getting down to the sharp end now and again to find out. Weak

135

enforcement is often the fault of managers who don't supervise their areas properly. But other policies have to depend on control systems that provide check-points to indicate if anything is out of line.

Sometimes it may be questionable whether it's worth having a policy if the system to regulate it is very expensive in time and effort. Perhaps the point of the policy isn't important enough to warrant it. Even if it is, maybe another rule could be established that would cover the point in a different way and one that would be easier to control.

The worst way to have to maintain a policy is to rely on 'making an example' of anyone caught overstepping it. Sometimes that may be the only possibility. But it will be seen as unfair and may not be all that effective. It doesn't make people concerned to avoid breaking the rule; it makes them careful to avoid being found out. If there's any scope for a more positive form to control, use it.

And the last of the five questions:

## 5. Are policies kept up-to-date?

Permanence as far as policies are concerned is a relative term. True, if it's worth making a policy on some point, it ought to be something that needs to be maintained over a period — otherwise why make a policy of it? But policies can't stay the same for ever. The *principles* they're intended to secure may not alter, but the rules themselves need regular revision.

Over time situations change, different needs become evident, new problems arise, old problems disappear. Think of the way organisations have strengthened their security policies over the past few years against the growing threat of bombings and hijackings. Think of the way their rules for the protection of their information systems have developed as computerisation has opened up new possibilities of fraud. Think of the tightening of personnel policy caused by the effects of employment and safety legislation. And the same thing happens on a small scale too. A policy you established six months ago might urgently need updating if today's needs are different.

If you're a manager who wants to stay in control, you don't expect your people to re-interpret your policies to suit the occasion. After all, a rule is a rule, not a general statement of what everyone will do if circumstances permit and if the weather's fine on Friday. You change the rule if it's no longer appropriate. But that implies that you notice when it *has* become inappropriate. At regular intervals you set aside time to review your polices to see whether any should be clarified, amended, updated, added to or simply scrapped. If they're written down, all of this is very much easier to do.

Throughout this discussion of policy, we've treated the question as a technical one: what rules are needed to enable an organisation to work properly? But sometimes there are bigger moral issues at stake. A company sets up a rule about confidential information to prevent its competitors from learning its business secrets. Having got the rule, managers apply it also to prevent information leaking out about company activities that could harm the public or land senior people in front of a court of law. A policy established for legitimate reasons can get used for other less laudable purposes.

Policy decided at a higher level can on occasions put the integrity of lower-level managers to the test, but the problem isn't always one of ethics. More often it tests a manager's sense of duty. If a policy your superiors have instituted impairs the efficiency or economy of your area or causes real injustice to your people, what do you do about it? Do you shrug your shoulders and take the easy way out — continuing to enforce a rule you know is a bad rule? Do you bend it where you've got a chance, in ways you know won't be detected? Or do you accept a responsibility to try to get the rule changed?

Every real manager *wants* his policies to be good ones. He wants them to work to the best interests of his organisation. Usually he also wants them to be reasonable for his staff and fair to any outsiders who might be affected — whether they're customers, suppliers or the public generally. But it's often difficult for him to foresee the full implications of a policy he's instituting. It's at least worth giving your boss the benefit of the doubt if he has introduced a policy that you can see is misguided. Quite possibly its purpose is sensible. He's trying to achieve the purpose in the wrong way — and doesn't realise the practical consequences that you're in a position to see. You're not being fair to him if you assume there's no point to the policy: you should at least try to find out what its aim is. But neither are you serving him well if you haven't the courage to explain to him the problems the policy itself is causing. In his place, wouldn't you want *your* subordinates to tell you?

Napoleon had similar advice for officers on the field of battle:

"A commander cannot take as an excuse for his mistakes in warfare an order given by his superior, when the person giving the order is absent from the field of operations and is imperfectly aware or wholly unaware of the latest state of affairs. It follows that any commander who undertakes to carry out a plan which he considers defective is at fault. He must put forward his reasons, insist on the plan being changed, and finally tender his resignation rather than be the instrument of his army's downfall".

Translate that as it might have been written for managers or supervisors who are subject to poor policy decisions made above them:

"A manager cannot give his superior's policies as an excuse for his own failures to manage his department properly, when the superior is often away from the department and doesn't understand the details or problems of its operations. If follows that any manager who undertakes to maintain a policy which he considers defective is at fault. He must explain what he thinks is wrong with it and insist that it is amended. In the last resort, he should be prepared to seek employment elsewhere rather than be forced to go on applying policies that are destroying the morale of his people or the efficacy of their work".

# F. Systems

Policies and systems are involved together in the way any organisation works. Policy says "do this" and a system says "in this way". Or a system tells you how to arrange a certain kind of activity and policy lays down rules to observe in operating it. Many systems are themselves matters of policy — the working of a budgeting system, a purchasing and stock control system, a work programming system. Other systems exist to enforce policy — disciplinary procedures, sanctions against misconduct, credit control drills. In fact many systems can't operate without policies to regulate them.

Yet organisations sometimes lack systems for their most basic needs — like a manufacturer of concrete beams and blocks in the North of England who was in financial trouble. Half his total operating costs were in payments for supplies of cement and other bulk materials. But he had no system whatsoever to ensure he'd really received what he was paying for. The surprising thing was *his* surprise when the audit required by his bank found a twenty per cent shortfall in his stocks of the stuff.

In other cases, control weaknesses aren't because of lack of a system but because the job a system was set up to do is 'mission impossible'. Such was the problem with the production control system in a Midland factory making electrical goods. All its products were manufactured in small batches to specific order, each one requiring several hundreds of parts to be bought in, machined and assembled. At any one time there were about fifteen hundred orders on hand. The production control system was supposed to channel all this work through the production areas — a foundry, a machine shop and assembly bays — to meet delivery deadlines and cost targets. The half million or so job tickets required to authorise, allocate and cost the work were filled in and shuffled around by an exhausted controller and fifteen overworked clerks, one ticket per machine or assembly operation per order.

A completed job ticket chosen at random showed two dates for the operation it covered: week 9 as the planned date, week 25 as the actual date it was done — sixteen weeks late. The clerk was unsurprised. He said that chasing orders was out of the question, he was far too busy keeping up with the paperwork. In any case he had no authority over the sequencing of jobs through the machines. The machine operators decided that for themselves as a means of regulating the pay they received through the piecework system.

There's a temptation to think this sort of system problem can be solved simply by the application of computerisation. The net result in a case like this is usually only to speed up the mess. The problem isn't a technological one; it's a failure of organisation and policy-making, itself often unwittingly caused by decisions taken by top management that are quite impossible to implement in practice. They expand sales, increase the product range, introduce new technologies, add further quality refinements and then fix deadlines and budgets by financial criteria rather than by operational practicalities. As a result the factory jams solid.

But the policy-makers don't take the blame. The senior managements who make the decisions that cause the mess aren't seen as the people who've failed. And everyone else who could possibly be involved in a peripheral kind of way is perfectly clear that the fault isn't his. You won't find an accountant who doesn't know where the cost problem is, or a head office that admits to total confusion about what's going on, or a design department that is uncertain about the way the product should look, or a union that's mixed up about its aims. It's always the factory that's wrong with its excessive scrap, idle men and machines, faulty products, late deliveries. The works managers and the superintendents, the production programmers and the foremen, the stock controllers and the sales administrators — they're the people who take the stick.

Perhaps in a sense it *is* their failure. If they alone can appreciate the real complexity of the production task, they have to be the people to explain it to top management: the sheer volume of detail involved in making the factory work, the fact that every machine breakdown, every absentee, every inspection failure, every change required by a customer or by a material shortage has its effects on the rest of the system and has to be managed. Unless they can get top management to understand what can reasonably be achieved, it becomes impossible to get the work done for the customers. Yet getting that work done is precisely what spells success or failure for the company.

The systems themselves can't be blamed for these sorts of difficulty which stem from failings in purpose or policy. But the way systems are designed and run can often create their own problems. In many a manufacturing organisation, for example, it is difficult to find out how the system that links sales, production, purchasing and distribution actually works — indeed it may not be understood all that well inside the organisation itself. Frequently the system is too complicated for the job it's intended to do. It operates in a sea of paperwork. When this is so, it is difficult to ensure the system is used properly.

Some years ago, a survey compared the features of good and poor production control systems in a number of similar types of manufacturing companies. It summarised the differences like this:

## Good control systems

Staff understood what the procedures were and what was being measured. They knew the implications of each thing they did within the system.

The systems required explicit lead-times to be allocated for paperwork preparation, purchasing etc. Assembly jobs weren't started until all materials and parts were ready.

Suppliers delivery performance was monitored and acted on. If it was poor and no other supplier was available, urging would begin well before the due date, and there was little reluctance to involve more senior management.

Routines were followed: documents were dated, entries were properly made, staff were concerned to keep the documents in order

There was a realistic appreciation of what could be achieved by when. Planned slack was left in forward programmes to allow for possible delays or over-running. Arrears were managed in a deliberate way.

## Poor control systems

Staff were frequently ignorant of the purpose of a document they handled. Jobs would be updated on the basis of rough guesswork about the consequences for work-flow.

The systems left out of consideration the timings for many necessary activities, potential sources of delay. Much waiting time was caused by assembly being started when parts were still missing. Long lists of shortages were a regular feature.

Deliveries were urged only when already overdue (some times excessively so). There was a resigned acceptance of poor delivery performance.

Disciplines were slack: documents often were carelessly mislaid or misplaced, entries were missing, dates were not quoted — or substituted by 'ASAP' (as soon as possible) or 'TBA' (to be advised).

Managers were generally over optimistic about what could be achieved within the time and capacity available. Arrears were commonly ignored until pressures made it impossible to do so any longer.

| Physical arrangements were as tidily operated as the control system itself. The place was kept clean, work-in-progress was neatly organised. | Housekeeping was often poor with cluttered floors and untidy work layouts. |
| --- | --- |
| Managers regarded the procedures as boundaries within which they were free to organise their operations to best effect. | Managers regarded the procedures as a constraint on their own freedom of action, to be ignored whenever circumstances gave them an excuse. |

Although these points were made about control systems in manufacturing companies, the principles they illustrate are true for almost any system for programming and controlling work.

Loose systems can create problems in control, but so can systems that are operated too restrictively. There was the case of the treasurer in a large municipal authority who had succeeded in gaining almost total power to approve or veto decisions in any of the authority's operating departments. As a result, the 'control' systems by which he kept himself informed of what was going on achieved more nearly the opposite of control. To operate with any degree of effectiveness, department heads and their officers had had to learn to manipulate the figures and statistics they were required to produce and to use fiddles to get round the treasurer's strictures.

In one instance, he had decreed that employees to be recruited for new installation operated by the authority must be hired at the bottom salary grade for that particular work. The people employed under this policy were too inexperienced to run the plant, but the treasurer would not be moved. So the officers responsible started rigging its staffing — hiring new employees according to the policy and then switching them with more experienced staff from other installations to get the new plant under way. Of course the figures and statistics and budget codings never reflected what was going on, even though the staffing patterns were continued year after year. The budgetary system actually became a device to conceal the facts. There was no real, honest or effective management control exercised by the treasurer, for all the data that his systems regularly collected.

142

Even when a system is officially in force, sometimes there's an unofficial system operating in defiance of the one laid down by official policy. It's not uncommon for it to be the more effective of the two. But if managers don't realise what's actually going on, some of their decisions can have disastrous consequences.

An investigation into an airliner crash discovered that the airline's official system of engine maintenance allowed defects in certain components to go unnoticed. It also found that until shortly before the accident, the maintenance engineers had operated an unofficial — and more thorough — system established by custom and practice. In this system the components at risk were automatically replaced during each engine overhaul. But the company had reorganised its maintenance department and had broken up the old maintenance teams. Many of the old hands had left, and the new teams weren't aware of the old practices — which had never been written down and were regarded even by those few managers who did know about them as unnecessarily cautious and uneconomic. Since the reorganisation, maintenance had been done according to the official system. The crash dramatically revealed one of the holes in it — at a cost of a hundred and seventy lives.

It's unlikely that many systems could cause a catastrophe on that scale. But that's no reason for allowing poor systems to continue wasting resources, squandering people's time,

143

producing meagre results and leaving managers uncertain about what's actually going on. Is anything happening regularly in your area of command that should be done systematically but isn't? Is there anything that ought to happen but frequently gets overlooked? Could the systems that do exist be more efficient: do they cause unproductive activity or leave you without proper control over important aspects of the things you're responsible for? Do any of them leave gaps — likely events that the system doesn't allow for? Might there be systems your people are actually operating that (like the airline managers) you should understand but don't? If you can't be certain the answer is 'No' in each case, does that persuade you to dig deeper?

To design a system, you need a method of charting that enables you to map out its stages in a visual form. For small systems, it's often enough to use a simple flow diagram: all you need is a brief note of what happens stage by stage in sequence:

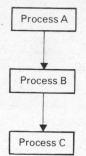

But many systems are too complex for such a simple arrangement. If they get different departments of the organisation doing different things at different times (and sometimes concurrently), you can't show what's happening by a single sequence of linked boxes. A more elaborate kind of chart is needed.

We'll end our discussion of systems with an illustration of how such a flow diagram can be laid out. It charts the purchasing system used in one organisation. The arrangement of columns, one for each department involved, is a good way of showing how the links in the system work. Also by looking down any one column, you can read off the list of actions for the department — a kind of 'system job description' for that department to perform.

144

The advantage of drawing up a flow diagram like this is that it makes it easier to check through the system for any weaknesses in the way it's designed:

- taking into account the volume of work that is processed through the system, can the staff who are operating it really cope with the workloads the system creates for them, designed the way it is?
- could any parts of the system be redesigned to cut out some operations or to make the links between them more straightforward? Could this reduce the number of staff needed to work it or the staff time it uses?
- do any operations need to be specified in more detail? Are people left to use their judgement over things that really need to be defined by subroutines in the system?
- should any operations be re-allocated between the departments or staff involved? Would it make the system more efficient to put together in one department some operations that are now divided between several?
- could any of the system documents be simplified to reduce the amount of time it takes to process them?

Besides its use in looking at questions like these in system design, the diagram has one further important value — simply as information for everyone involved in operating the system. Knowing how the bits they perform fit into the total system can help them use their judgement to better effect where judgement is required. No system can reduce to routine *everything* it involves. There always will be decisions to take at this point or that. Those decisions will be better made if the people taking them understand their consequences down the system line.

## System flow diagram

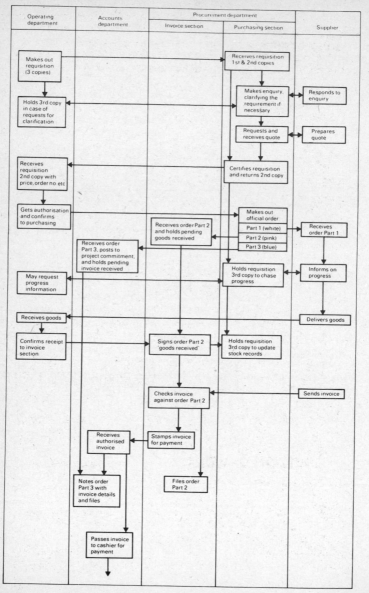

# Getting things organised

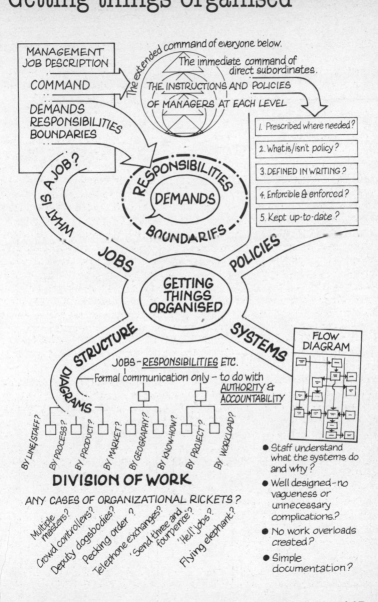

MANAGEMENT JOB DESCRIPTION

COMMAND

DEMANDS RESPONSIBILITIES BOUNDARIES

The extended command of everyone below.

The immediate command of direct subordinates.

THE INSTRUCTIONS AND POLICIES OF MANAGERS AT EACH LEVEL

1. Prescribed where needed?
2. What is/isn't policy?
3. DEFINED IN WRITING?
4. Enforcible & enforced?
5. Kept up-to-date?

WHAT IS A JOB?

RESPONSIBILITIES

DEMANDS

BOUNDARIES

JOBS

POLICIES

GETTING THINGS ORGANISED

STRUCTURE

SYSTEMS

DIAGRAMS

FLOW DIAGRAM

JOBS – RESPONSIBILITIES ETC.
Formal communication only – to do with AUTHORITY & ACCOUNTABILITY

BY LINE/STAFF?
BY PROCESS?
BY PRODUCT?
BY MARKET?
BY GEOGRAPHY?
BY KNOW-HOW?
BY PROJECT?
BY WORKLOAD?

## DIVISION OF WORK

ANY CASES OF ORGANIZATIONAL RICKETS?

Multiple masters?
Crowd controllers?
Deputy dogsbodies?
Pecking order?
Telephone exchanges?
'Send three and fourpence'?
'Hell' jobs?
Flying elephant?

- Staff understand what the systems do and why?
- Well designed – no vagueness or unnecessary complications?
- No work overloads created?
- Simple documentation?

147

# 5. Gettings things done

The biggest difference between a manager and a non-manager is in their understanding of what it takes to get things done. The non-manager will sit there in the middle of a situation that the manager has put a lot of effort into creating — the initiative for the decisions and instructions, the sheer hard *thinking* involved — and he'll take the whole thing for granted. It won't occur to him that it didn't happen of its own accord, that someone had to visualise everything that was needed, and then think through how to make all the actions happen that would cause that result to appear. He might carp at pretty little details he himself wouldn't have done just so. But he's quite unrealistic about it all. He doesn't notice whether or not the main thrust of the action has been in the right direction.

If he's an administrator type, the non-manager possibly assumes that systems and policies are somehow responsible for everything going on around him. That's *his* particular fantasy. Organisation can't get things done, any more that a road can make journeys happen. Structures, rules, procedures, systems — they're rather like building highways and bridges, creating traffic regulations, putting up road signs. They make it possible to get from place to place in good time and without risking life and limb. But the navigation and driving skills needed to steer each departmental bus have to be provided by its managers: keeping aware of where it's at, visualising where it ought to be by when, and reckoning how it can be got there in the time.

If you think all this is obvious, then why isn't it obvious to all those non-managers in managerial jobs? Because it clearly *isn't* so plain — judging by the number who'll commit themselves and their people to achieving this or that target without bothering to check whether it's possible, given the existing situation and the amount of work to be done. Then there are those who simply attend to things moment by moment without much thought beyond the immediate things they've got on hand — they muddle movement with progress, busyness with productivity. Others don't really know where they're at: instead of finding out the actual state of things on their patch, they're happy to rely on second or third-hand information. And the route maps used by many (their plans) are either hopelessly optimistic or else so sketchy as to be useless, often both.

Think of your management as a kind of bus-driver function:

**You need to keep your eyes open.** That's a matter of reading the information you're getting from control systems and from keeping in touch with things *as* they happen up at the pointed end — which are two different sorts of information. One is like looking at the map to check what was the place you've just passed through; the other is watching the traffic situation on the road at the point you've reached.

**You need forward vision.** Short-term and longer-term, you should have your ideas clear about where you're trying to get to — tomorrow, next week, next year even. When are you trying to get there? How will it contribute to the purpose of your department and even of the organisation as a whole in whatever market you're in? Besides that there's the question of where the road you're on is actually taking you — the siuation you're likely to find yourself in if you *don't* make any adjustments to your course. Forecasting and aim-setting are often confused with each other, but they're really quite different kinds of management activity.

**You have to try to anticipate events.** All management decisions and instructions are ahead of the action, but how far ahead? Possibly, many of yours have to be a matter of making up your mind on the instant about how to react to something that has just cropped up. But you make the action more effective whenever you can chart its route further into the future to avoid foreseeable difficulties, delays and accident risks. Good managers, like good drivers, don't let themselves get trapped by the problems that their less able counterparts crash into. They plan ahead to make the things happen that are likely to advance them nearer to their intended destinations.

## A. The open eye

The reason many managers don't feel they need to bother about working out aims and making plans is that they don't appreciate fully enough the situations they're trying to cope with. Of course they *know* in one sense or another what goes on — they're living with it day after day. But they're not actually applying the right questions to get an *understanding* of it.

If you don't understand where you are, there's not much point in trying to get anywhere else. You've no basis on which to judge the direction in which you should be moving, so aims and objectives become rather pointless. And if you haven't an aim it doesn't much matter where you are, so long as it's not somewhere you oughtn't to be. All you can do is to wait until something happens and then react to it as best you can — whether the 'something' is a requirement to get some work done, or a query from above about some costs that are becoming excessive, or an incident you've got to do something about. Nevertheless you're drifting. Instead of managing things towards a purpose, you can but treat demands, rules and systems as purposes in themselves. You can't have any real sense of personal responsibility for the direction in which the tide is taking your boat.

That's an overstatement of course. Every manager does have some idea of what he's up against in the situations he's trying to manage. But they're bound to be fairly complex, otherwise he wouldn't be required to manage them. So their control creates a bit of a problem for him — the huge amount of detail that's going on all the time, even in a relatively straightforward operation. In a department of any size it's impossible to keep tabs on all of it. Somehow the manager in charge of the thing has to simplify the moving picture if he's to manage it at all. He ignores a lot of what is happening ( it would be more accurate to say he doesn't try to find out) and concentrates on whatever he assumes is important at the time. What he *knows* is important, many a manager would say, but that's begging all sorts of questions.

It's common for managers to grapple with the problem in one of two ways. It depends on whether they are generalisers or detailists. Neither is a very effective method:

— the manager who looks only at generalities — the important things, he would say — disregards most of the hard facts that might raise doubts about his interpretations of events. He depends excessively on paper information and the figures in operational reports and financial summaries. (Though he *is* likely to be aware of priorities. Whether they're the right priorities is another question.)

It's deadly when a manager conceives of numbers as being more real than other kinds of information. They tell him a cost is getting out of line, but don't explain why. He sees that output is up or down, but has no real clues to show what is pushing it in either direction. Unfortunately the lack of facts doesn't disturb him, because he has got into the habit of regarding figures *as* facts. Naturally, he has to find some physical mechanisms to explain what's happening, but he interprets those from people's answers to his questions. He's not overly concerned to observe factual evidence.

Given the huge range of possibilities that lie in almost any practical situation, what odds would you place on the accuracy of his interpretations?

— the manager who watches only the details of what's actually happening in his area often misses the most significant things. Without the general picture he can't interpret them. Without the interpretation, he can't connect something he's seen here with another thing he noticed over there with yet a third thing he spotted last week... Because he lacks a sense of priorities, what he looks at doesn't tell him what he really ought to busy himself with.

The novelist Herman Wouk portrayed an extreme case of the problem in Captain Queeg, a character in his book ''The Caine Mutiny''. Queeg was a man so insecure and suspicious that he had to know every last detail of what every last tar aboard the U.S.S. Caine was doing in order to assure himself that all policies, rules and regulations of the U.S. Navy were observed in every trifle. His ship could be in the middle of a battle, but he had to complete his enquiry into who ate the quart of strawberries. What he and his kind forget in their pre-occupation with detail is that (a) they create a serious morale problem among the crew and (b) their ship becomes a liability to the rest of the fleet.

For good management you need *both* a wide-angle lens *and* the close-ups. On the one hand you have to see what's happening in specific, concrete terms — who's doing what, how, how often and why. On the other hand the summaries and figures you receive (or get together for yourself) tell you the way things are moving generally. Put the two together and the broad picture enables you to decide what to concentrate on, the detail keeps your feet on the ground.

If only that were all there is to it. The trouble is that it's not all that easy to see things for what they are. Even when we're looking at something going on, our minds unconsciously select particular bits of the scene to notice and remember. If we 'know' what's going to happen, we tend to see the things that confirm our expectations and not see other things that might conflict with them. And if we're committed to a certain view, we can even 'see' what was never there. If you want to comfort yourself with the thought that this is just psychologists' theory, you're right — it is. It also happens to be true.

A few years ago some research was done into the validity of evidence given by witnesses and the police during court hearings. Many groups of people were shown a film of an incident. Some of the people were police officers, others were members of the public — of whom half were told they would be witnesses for a 'prosecution', and the other half that they would be called for the 'defence'. All were asked to observe as factually and honestly as possible what actually happened. There was nothing they had at stake in the outcome, no difference in the way they were asked to report what they'd seen, so no reason to suppose they didn't try to do exactly that.

What the research demonstrated was that people differ in the types of thing they remember. Either they notice static detail (a person's height, clothing, hair and so on, the physical arrangement of objects) or they register actions (a person's movements and expressions, what he said, how something was done). Few were simultaneously good at both. The police — trained in observation — were very accurate on descriptions of the first type: on average they recalled twice as many points as the public. With actions the picture was reversed — who did what, said what. Here the public was better than the police, many of whom 'saw' things that hadn't actually happened.

But what was significant was the difference between the members of the public who'd watched the incident as 'defence' and 'prosecution' witnesses. Neither were more accurate than the other, but those for the prosecution were more like the police in their observations: there was a similar accuracy on detail and errors on actions. It seems that whether you're looking at a situation positively or negatively alters the kinds of thing you notice about the people and physical activities involved. Obviously this has implications for your attitudes as a manager observing things going on in your area. Management is generally more concerned with action and behaviour than with static detail. But if you're looking for culprits, you'll quite possibly 'see' things that aren't actually happening — and fail to see other things that *are* happening. Unconsciously your observations of the things that are most significant are more biased and unreliable.

Another problem is our tendency to stereotype things — to form fixed ideas about them that often don't correspond much to reality. This is more likely to happen if we're out of touch with what's actually happening. For instance, in organisations that deal with the public, many management decisions depend for their effectiveness on the sorts of assumption the managers concerned have made about the public. In practice, members of the public are endlessly resourceful in manipulating situations created by management decisions — more often than not, in ways the managers hadn't foreseen: they toss lifebelts into canals, spray warning notices with aerosol paints, read the contents of wastepaper baskets, fill in forms in all sorts of unlikely (i.e. unexpected) ways.

Yet managers — particularly senior managers — persist in thinking of the public as a simple, uncomplicated stereotype. They assume the public is well-behaved, sensible, literate, sober, of average build and height, possesses a good working knowledge of whatever their organisation deals with, and has an ability to suppress any impulses towards unconventional behaviour. Can anyone wonder that their staffs have trouble implementing the decisions based on such an idea?

Or take another example. Let's say you chair a regular committee meeting. You assume the more information you funnel to the members before each meeting, the better their grasp of the problems to be discussed. So they're sent a fat wad of working papers each time, a few days ahead of the next meeting. What's your stereotype of 'the committee member'? Someone who can and will take the time and trouble to read all the stuff, and who'll arrive open-minded but clear about the issues at stake?

That's not what actually happens. You ought to know it, but your stereotype blocks out the truth — and you're only human. Most of the committee members haven't the time or patience to read themselves to death just to find out what the problems are. They skip through the papers, reading bits only. Different members read different bits that imply different problems. One or two who do study them all carefully will feel they've fully understood the problems, and will come with solutions fixed in their minds. The others, thoroughly confused, will fall back on precedent or hunch — or be so open-minded as to have no mind on the matter at all. You get a lot of pointless argument and a bad decision at the end of it.

If you think the members are going to reveal all this in the meeting, you've got another think coming. *They've* got the same stereotype as you have about how they 'ought' to behave, so they won't let on about what's actually happening. Any self-respecting committee member with an ounce of savvy can put up a good enough act to leave you with your stereotype undisturbed.

There's yet a third problem: our proclivity for seeing what we want to believe. Often, believing is seeing, not the other way about. Let's take an educational example this time — a big survey that was conducted on behalf of one of the main

155

teachers' associations on opinions about standards in secondary schools. The survey showed quite sharp differences between the views of class-room teachers and those of the heads (i.e. managers) in the same schools. Two-thirds of the teachers believed general standards had deteriorated over the previous ten years; two-thirds of the heads thought they were about the same. Over half the teachers saw a decline in academic standards; three-quarters of the heads saw an improvement. Four-fifths of teachers said that discipline had grown worse; only just over half of the heads agreed with them.

*First question:* who is more likely to *want* to believe the best of the schools, the teachers in them or the heads who run them?
*Second question:* whose opinion is the more likely to be based on hard evidence?
*Third question:* whose opinion would *you* be more likely to trust?

People get used to seeing things in lop-sided ways. Coming from different parts of an organisation, they'll all see skewed pictures of the reality inside it. To the accountant, costs are real and anything that can't be summed up in figures is somehow less substantial. To the personnel guy, people's attitudes and abilities are real, things that don't count for much in the accountant's view of reality. The production man sees physical materials and processes as real, alongside which the customer's needs and interests are wispy and inconsequential. To the salesman the customer is the centre point to which everything else has to be made subservient — even the facts on occasion. There was this sales manager who persisted in quoting twelve weeks' delivery for a product that couldn't be made in under twenty weeks. When the backlog of complaining customers became too horrendous for his superiors to ignore, his indignant defence was that if he quoted twenty weeks he wouldn't get the orders! Many managers get themselves locked into such private idiocies.

What all of this suggests of course is that knowing (or rather thinking you know) what's actually going on in your neck of the woods is no insurance policy against doing something daft. You've also got to *understand* what's happening. And your understanding depends on the way you set about finding answers to three key questions:

- what *ought* to be happening?
- what is *actually* happening?
- where are the problems?

## Question one: what ought to be happening?

The answer may look easy. Policemen and witnesses *ought* to give the truth, the whole truth, and nothing but the truth. The public *ought* to behave themselves properly in their contacts with your organisation. The committee member *ought* to read everything he is sent in advance of the meeting. Headmasters *ought* to have an accurate idea of what's happening to the standards of education and discipline in their schools. All true. And all utterly impossible to achieve.

The same goes for operations that involve managers. All suppliers ought to keep their delivery promises. All stocks ought to be ready when needed for production or distribution. Every manufacturing process should be performed within time allowances and to high standards of accuracy. All systems should work smoothly and efficiently. No equipment ought ever to break down. Every salesman ought to sell effectively to each customer — who ought always to pay his bills on time... It can't happen, it would be ridiculous to expect it.

That's *not* what the question means. It's what ought *realistically* to be happening. You have to begin with a sensible idea of what, in this fallible world, it's reasonable to expect. What do you judge you might actually be able to get your department to achieve, given the conditions you've got?

It's a question of the way you establish your **standards**.

Now there's nothing very special about the idea of standards. We're all applying them all the time in our daily lives. It's just that we don't always *call* them standards. They are simply our idea of the way things ought to be. We have standards of living to try and maintain, quality standards for the products and services we buy, social standards by which we judge others' behaviour, standards for our own behaviour (what we call 'conscience'). Golfers have standards for their play — their handicap. Cricketers have standards for their game — their averages. The law represents standards of lawful activity, on top of which most of us have further standards of what we consider to be justice. The Ten Commandments are standards of religious obedience.

People's own private standards don't *have* to be sensible or rational. Many of them don't actually have much effect on what happens — they simply serve to make the people concerned either satisfied or dissatisfied about it: they produce grumbles, but little else. Others lie more in the control of the individual: they cause him to behave in one way rather than another, or to try to change other people's behaviour — he makes his dissatisfactions plain to them. Whether they take any notice depends on *their* standards. If they don't subscribe to his, there may be little he can do about it through normal social relationships. It's always possible of course that their standards will change, but then it's equally possible that he'll change his. Our standards do alter with time and experience — or even if we're pushed to think about them a bit, to try and justify them.

For the work you're managing, your standards *do* need to be rational because you've got the power to insist they're maintained. Your standards are whatever make you dissatisfied enough about this or that aspect of the work to get you *doing* something about it. Sure, you may see a lot of things happening in the organisation and even in your department that dissatisfy you, but that you reckon you've no hope of changing. You've standards for them right enough, but they're not really relevant to your management. You don't manage anything by standards that merely cause gripes and complaints.

The standards you apply are standards for your *responsibilities*. They're the ones on which you base your judgements about things you *can* control — whether directly or through your influence on other people: your subordinates, your colleagues, your superiors especially. You are bound to be applying standards of many different kinds to those things you feel you have some sort of management responsibility for:

| | |
|---|---|
| standards of results | How far do you judge your operation by the results it produces — rather than, say, by the effort everyone puts in? How well do you expect it to achieve what kinds of result: volumes, completion dates, cost limits, revenues, customer satisfaction etc? |
| efficiency standards | How quickly and smoothly do you expect operations to run? How timely and reliable do you expect the flow of information to be? What kinds of hitches, delays or backlogs would set you off looking for some way to improve the system? How do you reckon standards of efficiency? |
| quality standards | How do you define what 'quality' means in your area's output or in the service it offers? What level of quality do you try to maintain? If it began slipping, at what point would you start taking action? |
| economy standards | What kinds of waste would you notice in the use of time, materials, equipment, manpower etc? How much waste are you prepared to allow before you'll start doing something about it? (Don't say 'none': that's neither true nor practicable.) |
| performance standards | How do you tell how capable someone is in the different sorts of work you control? How capably do you expect each of your people to perform his work? (The standards will differ because you don't |

159

*expect* the same quality of performance from different people, do you?)

**standards of morale and discipline**

How do you tell the state of your people's morale? How do you know when it's beginning to fall — when it needs something doing to try to lift it? What kinds of behaviour do you notice as indicators of morale and discipline? What kinds of behaviour are you not prepared to put up with? Are you sure that's necessarily for the work — not just because you are getting over-sensitive or too easily affronted?

**management standards**

How do you judge the management performance of your subordinates who themselves have management responsibilities? What would dissatisfy you enough about their performance to take some sort of action?

Incidentally — how do you judge your own management standards?

**safety and security standards**

How do you identify the sorts of risks and hazards you want to know about? How do you decide when a risk is serious enough to warrant action to protect your standards?

**housekeeping standards**

How do you set the level of general tidiness you want to see around the place? What would make you feel that standards were slipping — that it was time to tighten the rules on getting mess cleared up, keeping things spick and span? What would you feel was overdoing it, making too much of a fad of tidiness?

This list can't be a complete one, but you get the idea? You do have standards for things like these, otherwise you'd never be dissatisfied with anything. But if you're like most managers, you've rarely tried to pin down in each case what precisely marks the point where you'd start doing something about it. It's just a feeling you've got for what's fair enough and what's definitely not on.

It wouldn't be reasonable to expect a manager to try and specify *all* his standards. Many of them may be somewhat nit-picking points, not terribly crucial to the operation he's running. But it *is* entirely reasonable to expect him to specify his standards for its key aspects. Consider what happens if you don't do this if you go on making up your mind on the spot about what is acceptable and what isn't, on the basis of standards you haven't really considered:

1. They're likely to be *variable* standards. Something you accepted last week without comment, you raise Caine about this week. If a standard is variable, it's the lower end of the range that always operates as the *real* standard. An occasional purge on waste or excessive costs doesn't actually raise the standard of economy. Once it's over, things are quickly back to normal, which is what standards are — what's normally taken as acceptable in each aspect of the work. However, you might try kidding yourself that your purge represented the real standard, which won't help the quality of your management.

2. There's going to be *uncertainty* whether you have or haven't got a standard for this or that aspect of your people's work. You leave them confused. If you can't explain to your subordinates the standards you're looking for in *their* responsibilities, if the only comment you can make to them is "I'll decide what I'll consider acceptable when I see how it's going", they can't really feel free to act. We're back to the question of job boundaries, because many of a manager's standards spell out the policies he expects his people to operate within. The boundaries aren't clear, so your subordinates can't be sure whether it's up to them to use

161

their judgement. That helps neither their morale nor their performance.

You might even be unconsciously operating double standards: you let the guy you like get away with things you won't accept from the fellow you don't like. That's simple injustice. If you let it go on once you've realised it's happening, it doesn't say much for your integrity as a manager.

3. Most damaging of all, your standards are likely to be *too low.* You may have none at all for quite important aspects of your operation — they've been allowed to drift. That can't have been helping morale any: people get apathetic working in an environment where anything goes, producing results they themselves can't regard as anything but mediocre. Low standards make your operation more of a liability than an asset to your organisation. Far more managements fail because they've been too complacent and easy-going about low standards of work than because they've set the standards too high.

To extract yourself from problems like these isn't exactly an overnight task. The first thing, and often the most difficult is to make out what *are* the standards you've subconsciously been trying to maintain. It begins with two questions on each aspect of your operation (aspects like those we listed a couple of pages back):

- how do you tell whether it's going well or badly? What do you look at? What signals are you reading?
- how do you decide 'this isn't good enough'? What questions do you ask yourself? What would move the read-out you're getting from no-action-required into a state where you're prepared to do something?

This isn't all that's needed, of course. The point of trying to establish what your standards *are* is to see where you should rethink them for the future. Where ought you to be more dissatisfied with things than you are? Where should you take action sooner — not letting things get into the state they sometimes do before you start to act? For instance, if you have no standard to distinguish what is an unacceptable level of machine breakdowns, perhaps you should have: what frequency of failures should start you getting dissatisfied enough to do something about it? Or rather than the number of breakdowns, is it the average downtime caused by each one that you should be looking at? Is that what you need a standard for? These are the kinds of question that attempts to sharpen up your standards will prompt you to ask.

Some of your standards you'll find can be expressed in **quantities** — you can put figures on them. Standards for results are usually the easiest to quantify, and often they exist already under a different name. They're called 'targets'. That doesn't alter the fact that they act as standards: if they're not met *this* month, there's a demand for management action to make sure they'll be met *next* month.

Besides targets, you'll find you can pin down figures for other kinds of standard you're operating. For instance, the frequency of something happening, whether you want it or don't want it. In a sales force you may judge your salesmen's efforts by the number of calls they make per day, the number of cold canvass calls per week. In a service operation, you might keep an eye on the number of customer complaints per period. In each case you have an idea at the back of your mind of the number that would suggest the sales efforts or the standard of service was slipping — it's a minimum figure in one case, a maximum in the other. But in each case it's *your* standard.

As a step towards control, you may sometimes need to set up a system that creates some figures. You intend using the system in the future as a control, but first you need to collect figures for a bit to see what is reasonable to expect. So for a month or two, you simply look at, say, the weekly figures for work volumes completed and the percentage of slack time. What you're doing is trying to work out whether it's possible to establish a quantitative standard and, if it *is* possible, where you might set the figure.

Where they *can* be used, quantitative standards have all the merits of measurement. They're objective; they can easily be adjusted; they are clear to everyone. But don't start thinking they're the only sort. For instance, you might keep an eye on the figures for staff absences to see if they relate in some way to the state of morale. Often there *is* a connection: if there is a continual high level of absenteeism in one section that doesn't exist in other sections, it may suggest a morale problem there. But morale itself isn't quantitative. Don't let the section leaders start to think that the staff absences you can measure are somehow more real than the morale you can't measure, otherwise they'll be tempted to try juggling with the attendance figures rather than tackling the real problem of poor morale.

Actually, most of the standards you'll be trying to pin down will be **qualitative**. There's nothing they give you to count. The

163

standard has to rest on your assessment of how things are going. It may be your reckoning of the quality of your area's 'product' or service — whatever it provides to others inside the organisation or even to your customers outside. Or perhaps it's the way you judge the efficiency and economy of your operation (though you can often get *some* kinds of figure to support judgements like these). Or it might be your assessments of your people's job performance and discipline. Look back at the various kinds of standards we listed a couple of pages back, and notice how many have got to be based on your personal judgement.

That doesn't mean that qualitative standards have to be uncertain. When your judgement is all you've got to go on, your people should at least know *what you look at and what questions you ask yourself* to make up your mind what is and isn't satisfactory. Well-judged qualitative standards are a precondition of good management in almost any part of the organisation.


## Question two: what is actually happening?

This is a question of your controls — the way you monitor things to keep yourself in the picture and to see whether standards are being maintained. Indeed, you usually need to have a pretty good idea of what's going on in your area as a whole before you can begin to make judgements about particular aspects of it. It's noticeable how, after most company take-overs, there's a period when the new bosses sit and apparently do nothing. Actually of course, they're sizing up what they've taken on. Before starting any moves, they want to be sure they can calculate all the consequences.

Non-managers often fail to appreciate the point of this. Richard Crossman was a Labour parliamentarian whose diaries raised quite a storm when they were published after his death, filled as they were with pungent comments about colleagues and civil servants he was involved with in the Wilson governments of the 1960s. But he himself was the subject of some fairly tart criticism from one of his senior civil servants, the formidable Dame Evelyn Sharpe. Writing about Crossman's approach when he took over the Ministry of Housing, she commented that he had never said "I'd better have three months to find out what the Ministry feels like and how it's accustomed to run" — if only to know how he might go about managing it. As a criticism of his management, that was pretty damning.

Even when managers realise how vital it is to get a picture of what's happening, they can still fail to get an *adequate* picture. Back in 1977 at a time when most of us were just beginning to hear the name of Michael Edwardes, the new man appointed to sort out the problems of British Leyland, one of the Company's executives throught back to a previous attempt to get the organisation working properly:

> "Ryder and his team of accountants and consultants crawled all over us for several months. Their efforts were largely treated as a joke and their questions answered largely from the top of the head. If Edwardes is to succeed, he will have to find out what is really going on..."

That Edwardes managed to do just that — where so many had failed before him — was a measure of his outstanding ability as a manager.

There are two ways a manager keeps himself in touch: by the *data* he gets from the organisation's INFORMATION SYSTEMS and by the *facts* he gets from his own DIRECT OBSERVATION. There's a notion that the first method is more appropriate for middle-to-senior managers, and the second for the foremen and supervisors. That the notion is popular doesn't alter the fact that it's dangerous rubbish. It simply means that a lot of British managements are content to rely on flimsy and inadequate controls. Every manager needs both data *and* facts — both paperwork *and* the knowledge he gets from personal legwork around his patch.

**Information systems** tell you how things are progressing generally — *if* they are well-designed to give you the sort of information you need and to avoid snowing you under with detail. With numerical data, however it's processed, does it actually mean something to you? Does it provide you with the means to get the answers to the questions you *ought* to be asking for the sake of your standards? Does it enable you to spot significant trends in the detail? For instance, it might indicate where a cost figure is beginning to get out of line, or show how some delays are affecting the overall picture of your results.

There may also be written information to help with the interpretation: summaries of sections' or departments' activities over the previous period, minutes of review meetings, working papers on investigations into this need or that problem. It's all

165

useful input into the longer-term thinking that needs to be done. A record of machine breakdowns may be essential information for improving the plant maintenance system. Its data may be invaluable in identifying common causes of breakdowns, and in evaluating the costs of breakdowns against the estimated costs of the preventative measures you're considering.

But there's another side to the picture. Too many control systems are too clever for their own purpose. There was the case of the insurance company a few years ago whose chief executive was committed to the idea of decentralising a previously highly centralised organisation. To give his regional executives the controls he reckoned were necessary, he instituted a sophisticated computerised system. It supplied them with every conceivable type of information they could ever want.

Each regional executive received every month a volume of two-hundred print-outs — standard data for all alike, most of it of only academic interest to him. He needed his own full-time analyst to identify what was relevant to his patch and to interpret the data into usable management information. The executive-analyst pairs became a standing joke in the company — an expensive joke for the company's staff costs.

All each executive actually *needed* was a short monthly digest of the specific pieces of management information from this total system that were relevant to his particular operation or department. With a bit of extra systems design, the existing system could have produced these digests. One sheet per executive per month; clearer understanding of what was happening; better management decisions; no analysts required.

Another, more fundamental weakness in information systems is that they can never tell you what's actually happening *now*. It's quite commonplace to compare them to the way thermostats work: the thermostat switches on the heater if the room temperature falls below a set temperature, and switches it off again when the temperature has been restored. Similarly the control system is supposed to alert managers if something is out of line, and to set them at ease if everything is shown to be in line. In fact it's a very bad analogy. Control systems deal in historical data, rarely less than a day old, and often as much as a week or a month old. They lay too much emphasis on the past, none at all on the present or future. They can hardly compare with the thermostat, which deals with instant information and takes immediate action — unless you can imagine a thermostat that turns the heat on and off a week late.

If information is bound to be late, you can often make it less late by being prepared to give up something on accuracy. Often a better control is provided by quick approximations than by fully-worked data that's going to take another three days to prepare.

Information systems, as we've seen, have some built-in problems. They frequently give managers far too much information about unimportant things, and their information is always out of date. But they have one further disability, and it's the worst of all. They say too little about important things. They can pump out great streams of useless numbers but still fail to point out the vital non-numerical fact that makes nonsense of the figures. In an international corporation, one division was buying iron ore from an outside supplier. It could have bought it from another division within the corporation for £1 million a year *less* than it was paying its supplier, but to do so the divisional director would have had to apologise to his opposite number for an error he had made five years before. That non-numerical fact was costing the corporation a highly numerical million pounds per year, but don't imagine it was recorded anywhere in the corporation's management information systems.

Apart from weaknesses of systems themselves, the information put into them can be distorted by human failings. Now and again it may be a case of a simple mistake: a sales clerk misreads a date or a quantity or a price from a sales ticket when he enters a transaction into the system, a production operative inadvertently puts a wrong job number on the works docket. But all systems are vulnerable to outright lies, too. The operative may deliberately hold back a few completed dockets to avoid any questions being asked about his 'excessive' earnings in a loose piecework system. The sales clerk might have discovered some fiddle that involves an occasional deliberate 'misreading' of a price. The fibbing may not even actually benefit the fibber very much, apart from saving him a certain amount of trouble. In one large factory, the shift foremen regularly recorded as the 'output' the figures that management had set as the target. The truth came to light only at stocktaking time — which is one of those occasions when facts *are* directly observed.

**Direct observation** is the only way you personally can get at the facts of what is happening *now*. Anything else is at best second or third-hand information on what might have been happening *then*. Whatever you are managing, to manage it well you need specific concrete details, not just generalities: what has gone out, when, to whom? How much have we got of this stuff? Who is doing this and why? How accurately is that being done? What's the reason for doing it that way rather than like this?... To get this sort of information, you have to see it happening with your own eyes — out there where the work is actually being done, whether that's in the office or plant or beyond, in the field of operations, in the branch office, on the work site. It's not just a matter of being present where the work is being performed. You've got to watch, listen, and think about what you're finding out.

This is not a popular activity among most managers above the supervisory level. What hobbles them more than anything else is their feeling that it's somehow beneath their dignity, their persistent belief that supervision is something for supervisors to do. The anxiety about communication you'll often hear expressed by middle-to-senior managers is often laughable coming from them — like someone who has avoided visiting his aged parents saying he is worried about the isolation of the elderly in our society. A consultant on assignment in a construction company described how concerned the members of its management committee were about maintaining the communication links required between construction sites and boardroom. Later during a visit to one of the sites he dropped into the foremen's hut for a cup of tea and a chat. The welcome he received was warm. He discovered he was the first member of management who had ever actually visited the foremen.

But there are many difficulties in the way of the manager who's trying to get at the facts. In some situations, it isn't a totally risk-free activity. Take the reception area in many service garages. Most car owners are familiar with the surly attitudes of service receptionists and the length of time it takes to get attention. The problems are usually due to poorly-selected, poorly trained and often poorly-paid staff, and the tidal nature of a reception area with long queues of impatiant customers night and morning and relatively little traffic in between. That the problems are allowed to persist unresolved is in turn due to non-managers up above, who have little idea of the scale of the problems — or find it more comfortable to ignore them. Little is likely to happen until directors and senior managers are willing to be present night and morning often enough and for long enough to get a real grasp of the problems — and brave enough to face their public. It's a crucial job which their status, privilege and other duties normally enable them to evade.

A second difficulty is in finding out when you *are* there what normally goes on when you're *not*. The fact you're present changes people's behaviour — which is why the well-advertised tour by a senior brasshat is so totally useless. Can anything he sees or hears be in any way representative of the normal state of affairs? If not, what's the point? There's no problem for the supervisor who's there regularly, but it gets increasingly difficult as you go up the hierarchy. To avoid having their efforts treated as V.I.P. visitations, managers at the middle-to-upper levels have to be sensible about the way they try to get facts.

It's a problem you'd think was even worse for television programme-makers who are trying to create a slice-of-life documentary. Yet they manage to solve it — like a programme a few years ago that took the cameras inside a typical secondary school. If the behaviour of the children and teachers had not been equally typical, the programme would have been pointless. To overcome the problem, the programme-makers and their equipment had to become invisible — not literally, but by being there often enough and long enough to become part of the furniture. When the cameras were eventually switched on, there was little argument that what the viewer was seeing was true: the noise of talking, laughing, shouting, wholly inattentive children was constant in almost every classroom scene. The teachers tried to teach through the racket, sometimes as if they had ceased to be aware of it, sometimes looking near the verge of a breakdown. If a whole camera-and-sound crew can find a way to observe real classroom behaviour truthfully, why is it that so many important people within the educational system don't seem to see what's actually happening in our schools?

The third difficulty with direct obervation is that the manager may find what he sees is rather upsetting. He may be tempted to ignore it, explain it away, or try to prevent others from seeing it. It says a lot for the integrity of the headmaster of the school used for the programme that he didn't try to stop it being screened once it became clear what it was going to reveal. He accepted that his school was typical of many ordinary comprehensives and said that, whatever his personal susceptibilities, he felt the film had to be shown, because it was true. "It deals with reality" he said "which is conspicuously lacking in almost everything written and said about education... These are the children we have to teach, whether we like it or not. And these are the teachers doing the teaching." To be fair to the manager, often the attempts to conceal the facts aren't down to him. They are those of other people — possibly his superiors, possibly outsiders with axes to grind — who are put out by his findings and who are trying to pressure him into silence.

There is one further difficulty: simply that the business of direct observation takes time. If you're running a department of any size, you're limited in the hours you can spend on any one aspect of its operations. But it's not impossible even then. Every week you can try to ensure that *some* part of your patch, no matter how tiny, gets from you enough concentrated attention to find out what's going on, what's going well, what's going wrong. And you try to pick the subject, place and time so that you're more likely to see samples of things that actually need your attention than samples of your own self-satisfaction.

To establish what is really happening, the information you get from your systems and the facts you get from direct observations have to be put together. Sometimes you might start observing something after you've been alerted to it by the system. For instance, take the way garage servicing and repair work is managed (or not, as the case maybe). The stories motorists tell of botched work are legion, but one manager in the trade points out that a lot of the problem would disappear if control procedures and personal supervision were properly integrated. It usually stems from bonus systems which give the mechanics an incentive to beat the times set for each job, leading to skimped work. If the work records indicate when jobs are consistently being completed in suspiciously short times, that ought to be enough of a hint to the managers concerned about where to concentrate their supervision. In other words, you notice something in the figures that suggests what you ought to look out for on the factory floor.

Just as often, it might work the other way round: you look at what's actually happening on the factory floor to see how to interpret the information you're getting from a system. This was the approach used by someone we've already mentioned — Leslie Chapman, the civil servant who conducted a campaign against waste in one region of a particular ministry, and who later wrote a devastating account of his findings in his book, *Your Disobedient Servant*. What subtle methods did he use to discover how public money was being squandered? Nothing very subtle really:

> "One afternoon in May 1967, in order to get some of the facts at first hand, I visited a depot near my regional headquarters without warning. I asked to see the records which showed how the directly-employed labour force was employed on that particular afternoon, what they were doing, and where they were doing it. Leaving aside those who were absent for one reason or another, about

seventy men were shown to be engaged in a variety of duties appropriate to a maintenance organisation. A great many of the duties were described in terms that did nothing to resolve doubts. While a few men were shown as doing a specific job, far too many others were engaged in duties described as 'general maintenance work' or 'routine maintenance duties'.

I decided to follow up this investigation by visiting a random sample of the jobs where the men were working. In almost every case the result was the same. Even the most useful work was of a kind which, in a commercial organisation, would have to be charged to overheads — tidying stores, sweeping and whitewashing. The rest of the work, and this was most of it, was nothing more than filling in time. I should add that a number of the men involved were stokers and boiler men and since this was warm weather with the heating switched off, the picture looked blacker than it would have done two or three months before. Nevertheless it was typical of the situation which was going to exist for the rest of the summer and in any case the stokers were not the only ones who were filling in time.

At the end of the afternoon, two conclusions seemed inescapable. In the first place, if this depot was typical, the amount of waste and overmanning was greater than anyone had suspected. Secondly, whatever the reasons might be and whoever was responsible for it, something would have to be done quickly to put this right''.

We've quoted from Chapman's book at length because he explains so clearly this approach to personal on-the-spot checking. You first look at the information in the system; you then go to find out what it means on the ground — and in doing so, take into account the kinds of practical considerations that systems often ignore (like the points about the weather and the time of year). This particular visit was the first step towards what eventually became a programme of investigation. Chapman himself accepts that his own first check was a superficial one. The later fact-finding teams he set up were briefed to be painstaking and thorough. But the principle was no different: to get the facts, you must directly observe what is going on. In this case the eventual result was to reduce the region's annual budget of £10 million by one-third — a saving of about £3½ million a year to the public purse.

The one thing you do *not* do is to confuse getting

information with acting on it. Too many managers are trigger-happy, rushing into action too early on the problems they think they see emerging from their control systems or their supervision. Whenever you spot a difference between what ought to be happening and what actually is happening, you have three options: do something, do nothing, get more facts. And that's their order of frequency for most managers, particularly with what seem obvious problems and easy decisions. More often than not, action is decided on the spot; quite often the problem doesn't seem all that serious so it's ignored; the last thing that occurs to the manager is that it might be worth finding out more about the problem. Yet at least half the time, the first need is to get more facts.

**Question three; where are the problems?**

Control is all about exposing what isn't going well in the light of existing circumstances. That's why direct observation is so important. A manager might well be able to see from the information he gets via a control system that something isn't going as well as it ought, but that doesn't necessarily say he has a problem there. 'In the light of existing circumstances' aren't empty words: it may well be that when he checks out the facts of those existing circumstances (i.e. actually gets off his backside and goes to look), he finds there isn't actually a problem — — or there *is* a problem, but not the one he was expecting to find.

172

Problem-spotting is a question of how you use the data and facts you've collected. It's not the automatic process many managers suppose it to be. A problem isn't always obvious at the point when a manager ought to be starting to do something about it. He has to try to discern the earliest signs of things going wrong, even recognise potential threats that have never happened — yet. He has to sort out real problems from imaginary ones, important problems from the less important, urgent problems from those that can wait.

Let's take a couple of examples of managers whose problem-spotting let them down.

**The manager who spotted the wrong problem**: he was an administrative director in a large food-manufacturing company that had established offices up and down the country to handle local sales and deliveries. The work in the offices was almost entirely clerical, but the jobs varied widely in difficulty and responsibility from simple typing jobs to complex transport coordination jobs. They were largely done by women — with the more able typists and clerks being helped to learn the co-ordinator jobs by the existing co-ordinators and stepping into their jobs as they left, which happened fairly frequently.

The fact that triggered the director's problem-spotting was the sudden resignation of two of the women coordinators at particularly unfortunate moments. In each case the reason was nothing out of the ordinary — one left to start a family, the other because her husband was being moved by his employer. But the resignations caused mistakes and omissions in the coordination work that resulted in serious complaints from important customers and the actual loss of some business.

What was the real problem? The fact that the office managers hadn't ensured the existing co-ordinators had understudies ready to replace them in just such an emergency.

What problem did the administrative director tackle? The fact that the staff turnover rate among women coordinators was inevitably high — about four times the rate among their male colleagues. As a result, he began a policy of appointing only men into the co-ordinator vacancies, and within a few years hardly any women coordinators remained.

This created a problem the manager hadn't foreseen. The jobs, though important, were not very stimulating. They were in fact dead-end jobs — there was little possibility of further promotion from them. This hadn't mattered to the women coordinators because they hadn't expected to stay with the company for a life-time. It did matter to the men. The result was a severe morale problem, a turnover rate among the male staff that rapidly approached the previous levels for the women, an increasingly militant work-force, and vastly higher payroll costs. The company paid a heavy price for its administrative wrong-problem spotting.

**The manager who spotted a non-problem**: he was a divisional head in a firm making machine tools. A minor modification had recently been introduced on one of the machines that had been sold by his division for several years. It had the effect of making the machine easier to operate, though no more efficient. Several hundreds of customers already had the unmodified model of course. The cost of installing the modification on new machines passing through the factory was negligible, although it was quite expensive to fit it on an existing machine. However, the company had a high reputation for the quality of its customer-care.

What was the real problem? There wasn't one. Existing users of the machine were generally happy with it in its unmodified form. Those few who wanted the new modification were quite willing to pay the cost of having it fitted. (These were the findings of some research done rather too late.)

What was the problem tackled by the divisional head? The fear that customer goodwill would be harmed when existing users of the machine discovered that an improved version of their machine was on the market at the same price. Without any evidence for this and without investigating the potential costs, he decided to install the new feature on all old machines cost-free.

The effect on goodwill was minimal. The cost-free fitting was certainly accepted by customers, but without any particular gratitude. As the size of the financial commitment became evident, more senior managers began to jib at the cost and the research was done. However it was by now too late to stop the modification programme, which had already been announced. That *would* have damaged goodwill.

These illustrations are of fairly high-level management decisions — a recruitment policy in the first case and a customer-care programme in the second. But the same principles can apply to the decisions taken at any management level. Even among supervisors there are no guarantees that their decisions always tackle real problems and the right problems.

The most common reason for failures in problem-spotting is that the problems are concealed or distorted by the very information that ought to be revealing them. Sometimes it's a case of a 'decoy problem' that obscures the manager's line of sight towards a real problem. And often enough it's the manager himself, his own psychology that gets in the way. These are some of the ways in which problems can get hidden:

## 1. The problem is 'hidden' by your own familiarity with it

Danger signals that would be spotted by new people in the department are often missed by the old hands simply because they've stopped noticing them. Here are a few of the sorts of things it's often worth trying to look at afresh:

- an arrangement of equipment or furniture that has been left untouched through several changes in the work, the workers, the way the work is organised.
- different arrangements of equipment or systems in different sections that do very similar work.
- a 'solution' to a workload or workflow problem that simply moves a bottleneck back up the sytem — or further down it.
- idle equipment or space in an otherwise busy area.
- difficult access to some parts of the area because work stations are overcrowded or poorly laid out.
- cluttered gangways, rubbish left lying around.
- careless treatment of valuable items of equipment, material, components etc.
- untidy stores areas, cupboards etc — useless or damaged materials left in them.
- a rising amount of waste of materials, or an increasing number of returns of sub-standard items from the field.
- a lot of reworking of work already done (for example by the bosses of the staff who did the work originally).
- people's manner — the attitudes staff show to

175

customers, the consideration with which they treat the public.

— suspiciously little difference in performance between new staff and the old hands. (The old hands should be that much more capable, but do they look like it? If not, you've probably got a problem with their motivation or their morale.)

## 2. The problem is hidden by detail

In any paperwork filing system, the document that's irretrievably lost is the one that's been put in the wrong file. A problem can similarly be hidden by getting itself buried in masses of detail, particularly irrelevant detail. The chances of noticing it become considerably less if the relevant bits of information are not all in one place.

The disaster the Americans suffered at Pearl Harbour in 1942 came about in just this way. The US military intelligence service had broken the top-priority Japanese code many months earlier. They *had* all the information needed to predict the Japanese attack and to prepare their defences in good time. But the relevant clues were scattered through the different files of the different branches of the service, and buried in details of other things that weren't relevant. They weren't spotted and put together — not unreasonably: they couldn't have *been* spotted until they *were* put together. The Japanese attack was unopposed.

## 3. The problem is hidden by generalisation

Local authorities who demolish houses that are perfectly sound are not generally regarded as doing the sensible thing — neither by the inhabitants whose lives are disrupted, nor by the ratepayers and taxpayers who have to pay for unnecessary re-development. Generally it's cheaper to keep those building that are sound, even in a terrace where other houses are in too poor a condition to be repaired. It also displaces fewer people, and prevents the whole neighbourhood from getting into that seedy, dilapidated condition that's called 'planning blight'.

Why then are sound houses often demolished? It's because local authorities tend to make their demolition decisions on the basis of large-scale surveys rather than by looking at the state of each individual house. A short time ago one of the London boroughs planned to knock down a complete street of twenty-three terrace houses. Normally that would have been the end of the matter, but on this occasion one of the owners was made of sterner stuff. A detailed survey was mounted. Its conclusions were that:

- six houses required no work at all.
- eleven could be put into perfectly good condition at the cost of a certain amount of improvement work.
- six were beyond hope.

The borough agreed to modify its original development plans to one of selective repair plus some complete rebuilding. As a result it saved £100,000 of public money, displaced only thirty residents rather than sixty, and completed the whole programme in two years less than the original plan would have taken.

If you try to spot your problems using only the large-scale sort of evidence you get from your central systems, you'll often put yourself in the position of the council that knocks down sound houses along with the unsound. You'll be changing some things that don't need changing. That's why it's important for you to go and see for yourself before you start making any big, sweeping changes. Just be certain you won't have lost anything valuable once the old ways have been superseded by the new.

## 4. The real problem is hidden by an apparent problem

In this case we have an example of a manager whose problem-spotting was successful. He identified a real problem concealed behind the problem that other mangers involved were busily hammering away at. He was a newly appointed sales manger in a cosmetics products company, who had taken charge of a region in which sales had been static for several years. This was despite a generous budget for the regional sales activities and a lot of effort by all the sales force to increase their market share. New customers could come only from competitors' market share, and the competitors had much the same idea. All in all, the different companies' sales efforts simply cancelled each other out.

The decoy problem, the one seen by the manager's predecessor and by the sales supervisors who reported to him, was a simple one of quantity: how many calls could each salesman make on customers of the competitor companies without neglecting his own regular customers? The answer, they had decided, was for salesmen to call on competitors' customers who were along their regular routes or who were close together in a particular location. That way they made the maximum number of calls with the minimum travelling time. They had a reasonable success in converting these prospects into new customers — about equivalent to the success of the

177

competitors' salesmen in doing the same thing. All the various competitors achieved was to redistribute customers among themselves — at considerable cost. Stalemate.

The problem spotted by the new manager was one of quality: how much business was each prospective customer worth? It was irrelevant how many prospects the salesmen called on. All that mattered was that they were ones that placed big orders: one new customer like that would be more difficult to win over, certainly but he would count for much more in increasing the region's market share than several smaller buyers put together.

So the sales supervisors were asked to identify the biggest customers of their competitors, and to estimate which were least likely to have strong ties with whichever competitor they bought from. Each salesman was given his priority list of prospects to visit, regardless of how much travel was involved in reaching them. The number of calls on new prospects dropped sharply, but the volume of new sales rose. Bigger new orders more than offset the continuing loss of small customers to the competition. At the same time the sales manager made certain that relationships with his own company's main customers were well cemented. The gains in market share were for the most part permanent.

The principles involved in this kind of thinking are ones we have already covered in the first book in this series, *What is a Manager?* They amount to changing your focus on the problem, and widening the field of your thinking. The change of focus here was obvious — the switch from the quantity to the quality of prospects visited. The field was broadened by removing the fence created by the idea of economising in travel time. Once that was down, the way was clear to a successful campaign for new business.

## 5. The problem is hidden by the manager's own psychology

When people are first presented with clues that something is going wrong in a situation they feel very familiar with, their reactions are usually predictable. This is particularly so if:

    a) the clues aren't absolutely conclusive,
    b) recognising the problem will involve a certain amount
       of inconvenience.

They discount the threat. Certainly they are reluctant to call for help, even if the problem is one that could place them in considerable personal danger. One-sixth of the fires attended by fire brigades get out of control simply because of delay in calling the firemen.

A manager isn't different from anyone else in this respect. Perhaps it's wrong to say the problem is hidden. It's more that he doesn't properly grasp the significance of the clues he is getting — and will even try to calm the fears of others who *are* alarmed by them. Even if he does have an inkling there's trouble afoot, he's still faced with a dilemma:

- if he ignores the clues, he can't prepare to cope with the possible emergency. It may then be far more difficult to handle once it actually happens.

- if he reacts too quickly, he might be putting himself to a lot of bother for something that turns out to be a false alarm. There might be other effects too in the costs and general disturbance caused by his unnecessary action. Sometimes the very fact he has recognisd the threat increases the likelihood of its materialising — particularly if it's a question of people's behaviour. For instance, police preparations to deal with the risk of civil disturbances can make the disturbances more likely, not less likely, to happen.

The point of realising that we do tend to play problems down is to be forearmed to deal with the tendency. If it's a question of this tendency in yourself, try to allow for it in your own problem-spotting. If it's more a matter of attempting to cope with it in other people, accept that you might sometimes have to overstress a risk to get it recognised at all.

We've called the whole of this aspect of management — knowing what ought to happen and what does happen, and then problem-spotting among the differences — the Open Eye. There's another sense-organ that's equally important: the Listening Ear. If you keep that particular orifice clear, there's no shortage of critical voices to help pin down the real problems that should be engaging your attention. Customers, competitors or the long-suffering public; subordinates, colleagues or consultants — they can all add their pennyworth. But the real question is which of them are the most worth listening to. Managers tend to lend an ear in inverse proportion to the toughness — and therefore the value — of the criticisms they're likely to get. The toughest critics and the most useful are usually those given least attention:

- dissatisfied customers, including the public your outfit deals with. The wretched people are doubtless always wrong in one way or another, but that doesn't mean their complaints can safely be ignored. There may be no problem where they say there's one, but it's a pound to a penny there *is* a real problem somewhere round there.

— talkative competitors. If they've spotted a weakness in your product, your service, your selling methods or your marketing systems they won't keep quiet, the idiots. Your organisation can benefit from their free information.

— disgruntled subordinates, including ex-subordinates. Often they can offer the most pointed help of all, but it's going to be uncomfortable listening — the very sort of listening that's necessary for problem-spotting. It's no argument to say they're biased *against* whatever is going on: anyway you're biased *for* it so you need some kind of counterbalance to that risky and occasionally foolhardy optimism. Learn to listen without fighting back. A lot of what you hear will inevitably be worthless, but now and again you'll pick up a pearl. Mud-covered it may be, but it wil come at a price far below what a consultant would charge for the same thing nicely wrapped.

## Forward vision

A captain who navigated his ship by peering over the stern-rail at its wake wouldn't retain his master's ticket for long. He can't set a course and avoid the hazards of rocks, wrecks, storms, other shipping and suchlike nautical misadventures simply on his knowledge of his vessel's past progress and present whereabouts. The idea is to look for'ard as far as possible using eyesight, binoculars, radar and any other aids going. Obvious for navigation. Not so often applied in management. Foresight isn't a noticeably powerful feature of a lot of managers' thinking. Instead they persist in concentrating on the data provided by their control systems — by definition, information from the past — and seeking therein some inspiration for their decisions — again, by definition, for action in the future.

This is a ludicrous situation. Yet it happens again and again in operations that are supposedly being 'managed'. So there must be some compelling reason for managers preferring hindsight to foresight. It's possibly because hindsight makes experts of us all: it's detailed, firm, precise — and assuredly correct. It's also totally pointless by itself. No one can remake the past. Foresight on the other hand is undetailed, shadowy, imprecise — and just as assuredly incorrect to a greater or lesser extent. It's also totally necessary for any sort of management worth the name. This doesn't deny the value of your knowledge and experience of the past, but equally they're not much good unless you can interpret them into ideas about the future.

For you as a manager, the point of your knowledge and experience is to help your imagination better conceive of possibilities in the future and to work out how you can cope with them or work towards them. But what sorts of knowledge do you need? Not just a narrow expertise in your own operation. To avoid getting trapped in mental tramlines you also need an enquiring mind, a wide range of interest, an acquaintance with functions other than your own. Even an inkling of how other organisations in different fields operate can be valuable. It's all fodder to fuel your imagination. Then there's the way you use your mind — your ability to explore unconventional lines of thought on familiar themes, to look at things from varying angles, to develop innovative ideas about the activities you're managing. "Imagination" said Einstein "is more important than knowledge". The test of a manager's calibre is the kind of vision he can create for the future of whatever he's running, and the imagination and guts he applies to making it come true.

The closer you are to the top of the organisation, the more important do these traits become — simply because your vision has to reach that much further ahead and the size of the canvas is that much larger. So how do top managers rate their importance? The Institute of Directors invited some seventy chairmen and chief executives of major public companies in the U.K. to declare their views in a survey the Institute conducted. Each one received a questionnaire that listed a variety of personal qualities that could be considered relevant to management generally. He was asked to pick out those he considered important in the management of his own organisation. Four of the qualities included in the questionnaire are below: alongside each is the number of captains of industry who included it among their choices:

| | |
|---|---|
| Knowledge of own business | 24 |
| An enquiring mind | 2 |
| Ability to innovate | 2 |
| Knowledge of other businesses | 2 |

If these are the views of the men at the top, what of those below? Perhaps there's a clue here to why huge tracts of British management so closely resemble the Gobi desert for fertility of thought.

Forward vision has to *begin* from the point where you are. It can't be realistic without the knowledge of actual events, results, methods, problems and performance that you get from your controls and your supervision. You have to know your starting-point before you can work out the directions in which you might move. But from then on, there are two tasks that call for something more than simple knowledge: FORECASTING and AIM-SETTING. Both are exercises in imaginative thinking, but different exercises. One envisages the course of future events and calculates (or *ought* to calculate) their likelihood; the other decides how to take the best advantage of them.

## Forecasting

Don't get the idea that in management the only sorts of forecast worth the name are those long-term predictions made by economists and corporate strategists and marketing researchers and people of that sort. If you've an idea that something is likely to happen in the next few weeks that will affect the operation you're managing, that's just as much a forecast as a prediction about when the world's oil reserves will be exhausted. For you it's a more important forecast because it will influence the decisions you make in the light of that idea. You're not likely to be able to do very much about the oil problem. The point of making a forecast isn't to see how clever you are at making predictions, but *to enable you to make better decisions.*

In fact there's an even more fundamental point. It's a common human tendency to assume that things will be exactly the same tomorrow as they are today and were yesterday — whether 'tomorrow' means literally that, or in a month or a year's time. We even miss the differences between yesterday and today. If you've been involved continuously in a situation, it's often difficult to see how it has changed from the way it was, say, six months ago. By degrees it might have altered a lot over that time, but a steady shift is something we tend not to notice. Someone who has been out of the situation for that time and then comes back into it *does* notice the differences, but you're quite likely to think he's exaggerating or imagining them.

There's a risk that the manager won't spot a trend even when it represents a growing danger — or alternatively opens up the opportunity to do something that wasn't possible before. Managers are frequently caught out by sudden emergencies that shouldn't have been so unexpected. Take the case of the recession that began during 1979 and 1980 and one of its effects for local newspapers. Until that time one of the major sources of their revenue was recruitment advertising — the page after page of 'situation vacant' notices they used to carry until the recession began to bite. The recession's timing and its severity had been forecast for several years, reasonably accurately as it turned out. But few newspaper managements seemed to have seen one of its implications — the effect on their advertisement revenue of the soaring unemployment it was due to cause. At any rate, few were prepared for what was about to happen. At the beginning of 1980, recruitment avertisement sales targets for the year were still being set on the time-honoured basis of 'last year plus five per cent' or whatever. When the bottom suddenly dropped out of the market around May or June of that year there was a scramble to cut costs, reconstruct the targets, redraft budgets — not the best way to arrive at effective, well-judged decisions.

There are also the opportunities that get ignored. Managers will go on insisting that this or that improvement is impossible to achieve, on the grounds that it wasn't possible a year or two ago. They don't look for the signs that the door has since been unlocked. A change in their organisation could have done it — new people, new policies, different pressures; or a change in the market — new interests, new concerns, different demands; perhaps even a broader change in the general social climate of opinions and attitudes. Even when a colleague demonstrates that a change can be made, they'll still deny the possibility for themselves. There was this newly-appointed department head in a Manchester company who fought the rule — long established in the department — that the union decided who was to fill each job vacancy on his machines, whether the card-carrying members they sent were competent or not. He had realised that times had changed and that the union could no longer insist that he accepted whoever they sent. Yet the heads of other departments in the same situation continued to believe, despite the evidence, that the old custom was something they could 'never' alter.

Forecasting tries to counteract this blindness to change. But there are forecasts and forecasts, depending on what they are trying to predict, the purpose of predicting it, and the probability of the predictions coming true.

## 1. Weather forecast or earthquake forecast?
In other words, is it trying to predict changes and developments in the manager's environment as a basis for his planning of operations, or is it trying to estimate the likelihood of

catastrophes that can be cushioned, deflected or insured against?

Think of the ways a real weather forecast is used by farmers and fishermen — or, for that matter, by the transport or construction industries. They can't avoid the weather, even though it can have quite crucial effects on their operations. But their planning is easier and their decisions likely to be more productive if they know what to expect. They can even take steps to reduce the problems and losses that might be caused by bad weather.

The same applies to forecasts about market trends, product sales, price movements, employment patterns, availability of funds, economic conditions and so on. They're all 'weather prediction' types of forecast. Like weather forecasts they need to be reasonably reliable on what is going to happen, *when*. A weather forecast would be pretty useless if the forecaster couldn't tell you whether it was for tomorrow or the day after. And although ideally you may want to look well into the future, you have to accept that any attempts to make precise forecasts about the long-term weather are likely to be less and less accurate the further they are ahead. We'll come back to this problem later.

Earthquake forecasts are different. The point isn't to be exact about timing but to be pretty accurate about the *probability* of something happening within a given time. The further ahead the forecast looks, the better the chance that the quoted probability is accurate. The purpose is usually to calculate how much money or effort it's worth spending, how much trouble it's worth going to in order to limit the damage that could be caused. And if large amounts of money or effort or trouble are involved, accurate assessment of the probabilities is important. Commonly these sorts of forecast are called *'risk assessment'*: the risks of fire or flood, of building or bridges collapsing, of explosions in chemical plant, of escapes of dangerous materials, of accidents in the home or work-place. They're all 'earthquake prediction' types of forecast.

The difficulty with risk assessment is that often it can't be entirely objective and logical. People's feelings come into the picture. They get more concerned about the prospect of a man-made disaster than a natural one: the risk of, say, a coal-tip sliding down a hillside is more disturbing than the risk of an earthquake, just supposing that the two had exactly the same probability of actually happening. In other words, there'll be a demand for fuller, more costly precautions against the threat

185

from a coal-tip than against the threat from an earthquake. Perceptions of risk are subjective. If someone is hit by a stick, there's a real difference between his finding that it fell from a rotting tree or that it had been carelessly tossed away by someone else.

This is why the management of risk is so controversial. People's prejudices and gut feelings have to be allowed for, but sometimes things can be taken to ridiculous and wasteful extremes. There was the case of an asbestos scare caused by a couple of isolated incidents in schools in Liverpool. As a result, every child who had attended any Liverpool school over the previous five years was X-rayed. Yet the cancer risk from the X-rays, though small, was significantly greater than the risk from the asbestos. Also the cost of the whole programme would have served Liverpool's health better it if had been spent on *real* patients. Common-sense often takes a back seat in decisions about risks, real or imagined.

Perceptions of risk are also easily influenced by political and social pressures, and by what newspaper editors and television people consider newsworthy. Sometimes the resulting costs to both private and public organisations are quite disproportionate. After the disaster at Ronan Point — the block of flats that partially collapsed after a gas explosion, killing several residents — building standards were changed. Taking into account the extra building costs created by the new standards and the lives that were calculated to have been saved, the changes implied that the value of a life was £20 million. Contrast that with the fate of a proposal to introduce checks on the hormone levels of pregnant women throughout the country. The estimated cost would have been £50 for each still-birth avoided. The proposal was rejected. As someone remarked at the time: ''people strongly object to being blown up in their homes, but they don't regard unborn babies as members of the human race''. Brutal but true.

People select and distort what they attend to (where have you heard that before?). They take more notice of an air crash that kills a hundred than a equivalent death toll from a week's road accidents. They are more sensitive to the risks in some industries than others: mines have to be safer than farms before the public *feel* they're equally safe, yet agriculture is one of the highest-risk industries there is. Some kinds of risk become phobias in the public mind: perhaps you still feel that Liverpool was right to treat a slight risk from asbestos more seriously than a greater risk from X-rays. But then asbestos rings alarm bells that don't respond to comfy old X-rays — unless you call *them* 'radiation'.

Managers often feel that it doesn't matter if precautions *are* taken beyond the demands of logic or reason. ''They may cost rather more'' is a common line of argument, ''but it's worth it to allay people's fears''. Quite apart from whether the costs would be better applied to *real* improvements in safety, the argument is often false. Risks can actually be increased by incorporating more and more unnecessary precautions and safety devices. Each one adds its quota of further complications that introduce new and unrecognised risks — like the X-raying of Liverpool schoolchildren, or the vent pipe that nearly caused the loss of a ship. It had been installed to prevent a build-up of dangerous gases in her battery-room. Its designer failed to appreciate the potential of his vent to create new risks of its own: it provided not only an escape for gases but also an entry for seawater. When the ship first ran into heavy seas the battery-room flooded, crippling her electrical system. And there's always the discomforting thought of the ship that was supposed to be unsinkable — the 'Titanic'. People may fail to respond with enough speed and decisiveness to a real danger if they are foolishly persuaded that all risks have been covered. The effect may be to deaden their feelings of personal responsibility for exercising care and good judgement, and their sense of urgency if something *does* go wrong.

Curiously enough, when it's to do with something under their own control, individuals more often *under*estimate than overestimate a risk — particularly if the situation is a familiar one. Riding a motor-cycle, crossing a busy street, climbing a ladder, using a potentially dangerous piece of equipment — whether it's a hedge-trimmer in the garden or a lathe in the workplace. Even though an activity involves a considerable potential danger to life and limb, human beings have a strong tendency to pride themselves on their skill in handling the risk and to believe in their own invulnerability. In view of the enormous range of hazards that lie in the path of almost any everyday activity, this optimism may be just as well. It enables people to get on with the task in hand without worrying about all the things that could go wrong. But it's yet another factor a manager has to bear in mind: he can't depend on his people's estimates of the risks — he has to make his own mind up.

What does the question of risk assessments — 'earthquake forecasts' as we've called them — imply for your management? The point is to try to be realistic. Being rational about it, how much of your attention is deserved by each of the different potentials for calamity that exist in the operation you manage? How much damage could they do to your organisation? How serious are the risks they create for the people involved? How likely are they to happen? You can't belittle people's personal anxieties even though you may sometimes feel they're overdone; at the same time you have to make some attempt to reckon other risks that your staff may be too casual about. What is needed is a balanced view on the amount of time, effort and money each risk warrants spending, and the total benefits you get in terms of the security of your operations and the safety and morale of your people.

## 2. A forecast of trends or events?

Let's return to the 'weather forecast' type of prediction we mentioned earlier. There are two kinds of this sort of forecast. One looks back at records of past weather conditions, average sunshine hours, rainfall figures, prevailing wind directions and that kind of thing, and attempts to spot trends that can be extended into the future. In other words it's a forecast based on numbers, frequencies, deviations, percentages — all quantitative data of one sort or another. It's produced by manipulating figures and statistics. It predicts whether summers are getting warmer or cooler, winters are getting wetter or drier, snowfalls are more or less likely. That's a forecast of trends.

The other kind of forecast looks at the weather you've actually got, reaches back into experience for recollections of similar patterns, and tries to make sense of hints and suggestions from all kinds of country lore — perhaps the behaviour of birds and insects, peculiarities in plant growth, even personal intuitions, who knows? It comes up with predictions about what next summer is likely to be like, or when we can expect the first frosts next winter. It's a forecast based on qualitative information for the most part. It tries to build a likely story or 'scenario' for the way things could turn out. That's a forecast of events.

Both kinds of forecast have their equivalents in the ways managers try to estimate what the future might hold in store. Of the two, trend forecasts have a better record of reliability, even though careful calculations do sometimes prove no more accurate than the hunches of wise managerial heads. Whether they are attempting to predict what is likely to happen in a market, or the stock-levels that will be needed for different items, or the way price changes will affect sales volumes — they are all based on certain mathematical principles and techniques.

The forecasters can construct graphs from the historical data created by control systems, recognised the patterns followed by the trends depicted in the graph lines, and extend the lines into the future, often with uncanny accuracy. They can also calculate the likely margin of error — how much reliance can be placed on the trend forecasts. As long as the numbers are large enough. The larger the numbers, the more reliable the predictions. So trend forecasts depend on your having a lot of figure-work from your records to use as the raw material for your forecasting methods. The date and statistics from control systems do have some important parts to play in longer-term decision-making and this is one of the main ones.

But it's a different story when you're trying to forecast events. Few things make more fascinating reading than looking at what forecasters have predicted in the past and comparing their predictions with actual outcomes. The faster-changing the business you're in, the bigger the divergencies.

Here for instance are four predictions made in 1967 by a group of experts about events in computer developments over the following fifteen years. Against each you'll see what actually happened.

| Prediction | Outcome |
|---|---|
| By 1975 large shops and stores would have direct computer links with banks to check credit and to record transactions. | A considerable overestimate. Only in 1983 were such links for credit checks being installed. No transaction recording systems were operating. Even by 1984 they were still only at the experimental stage. |
| By 1978, libraries would hold texts of books etc. in computer files and reproduce them as required. | No such thing had happened by 1984. Though technically possible no move had been made towards automatic libraries. |
| By 1979 there would be ten fully integrated computer-based management information systems operating in the U.K. | No fully integrated system existed in any sizeable organisation in 1984. There were many management information systems operating, but their levels of integration were far lower than the experts had confidently predicted. |

| Possibly by 1984, processor chips would become available with 10,000 transistor elements to the square inch. | A vast underestimate. In 1982 a chip of considerably less than an inch square containing 450,000 elements was in full production. |

The interesting thing about this set of predictions is the kinds of thing they over- and under-estimated. Forecasters consistently under-rate the power of *social* and *economic* factors to put brakes on the speed of change (the first three predictions above). Conversely, they typically over-rate the difficulties of solving *technological* problems (the last of the predictions).

Just because something *can* be done doesn't mean that people will *want* to do it that way. If they don't see a big enough advantage in it, if it seems too expensive, if it upsets comfortable habits, the technology won't get used. In fact the biggest miscalculation the computer scientists have made (and are still making) is in underestimating how complex human beings are — the processes involved in thinking, learning and understanding things. In 1964 an IBM expert predicted that the problem of designing computers that could learn would be solved well before 1984. But in 1984 their guesswork was that it would be done in another ten years. Well — let's wait and see. It isn't a problem of the technology involved but of understanding the processes the technology is trying to imitate, the tremendous complexity of the human brain.

With technological predictions, the underestimates may be easier to explain. Forecasters who are themselves technologists presumably respect the immense problems involved in making advances in their technical fields. It seems to be a general human characteristic to be cautious, even pessimistic, in prophesying changes in things we know about and understand. With things we don't really understand, we feel we can safely ignore the difficulties involved. What we don't know doesn't bother us, and we rush into blind optimism.

With this in mind, here are four rules for forecasts, not altogether tongue in cheek:

1. The one certain thing about any forecast is that it will be wrong. The further ahead it is for, the wronger it'll be.
2. Once a forecast has been made as accurate as possible, calculate how wrong it's likely to be. If you can't do this, the forecast is worthless. Also you're likely to learn as much from estimating its margin of error as you did from making the forecast in the first place.

3. If you still intend taking the forecast seriously, study the *effects* of getting it wrong in different directions and by different margins. What differences will they make to the practicability of any plans you're drawing up on the basis of the forecast?
4. If the forecast is one you've received from someone else, don't even think of acting on it until you have enquired about the forecaster's track record with his previous forecasts.

## Aim-setting

Aims and forecasts are *not* the same, of course. A lot of managers who should know better still persist in calling their objectives 'forecasts'. In fact there's a hell of a difference, managerially speaking:

— your *forecast* is what you think is going to happen anyway. Your efforts won't have anything to do with it. Whether or not it comes true is solely a question of the judgement, intuition or whatever you've used to arrive at your prediction — possibly the quality of your crystal ball.

— your *aim* is what you intend to try to make happen. Your efforts will be all-important. Whether or not it *can* come true is a question of your judgement in setting it; whether it *does* come true is to do with your skill and determination to bend the course of events that way.

The point of having an aim is that it creates a reference-point for each of your day-to-day decisions. You can ask "what scope does this decision give me to push things further in the direction I want them to go?"

Without an aim, the question is meaningless. Each decision has to be taken on the basis of whatever seems a good idea at the time. The manager has no consistent line against which he can judge the questions he has to deal with. He either seeks to maintain the *status quo,* or he operates arbitrarily and mechanically. He follows the system rigidly, whether or not it's appropriate to the particular case he's dealing with. He gives obedience to instructions and policies a higher priority than the results that are achieved. He becomes absorbed in the narrow technical details of his tasks and loses sight of their broader implications. He has no problems — since a problem is the difference between where you know you are and where you think you ought to be. It implies an aim.

Question such a manager about his aims and he'll still have answers of a sort, but only because he feels he's supposed to have them, not because he has a personal commitment to achieving something. They won't be aims that convince you you're talking to someone with a dynamic sense of purpose:

- "I see my aim as organising my team to achieve the targets we're given by my superiors."
- "My job has various aspects, but the real point is to see that everyone in the section does what they're supposed to do."
- "What I'm here for is to make sure the office runs smoothly."
- "My aim? I suppose it's really to administer the department as efficiently as possible."

Aims like these say little. No, that's not precisely correct. They do say quite a lot about the way the manager concerned understands the word 'aim'. He's confusing it with tasks, things to do, obeying policies, minding the shop. Compare those statements with the sort of talk you hear from managers who have thought about what they are trying to achieve:

- "The quality of our work is my first priority. Ideally it ought to be 100% accurate — and without running into problems of overdues and broken deadlines. I don't know whether we can ever achieve that totally, but we're making progress steadily in that direction."
- "We're going to get a big increase in our workloads over the next six months, which is going to mean some reorganisation to handle it. My intention is that our existing staff cope with it all, without any backlogs building up."
- "I'm constantly trying to keep my staff interested and involved in what we're all doing together. That's the only way I know to ensure that our public feel really satisfied with the treatment they get."
- "Our objective for new business is to secure twenty new customer accounts in this area within the next three months."

Each of these declares a commitment to getting somewhere that will demand effort and imagination from the manager and his people.

The sense of personal commitment is a vital part of an aim, which is one of the things that makes it different from a policy. 'Aim' is the direction in which you've decided to make a stream of action and decision-making flow; 'policy' establishes where the banks of the stream lie. If you are operating on targets that are handed down to you by your boss, the targets may genuinely be aims for him — he has worked them out himself, is emotionally involved in making them come true. They're policies for you. You can't feel a personal commitment to them yourself unless you've had a hand in shaping them. *Your* aims for your area are directions of movement for it that *you* have either worked out yourself, or at least taken part in working out.

There's quite a bit of confusion over the different kinds of aim that exist. Many managers, for instance, would say that the four aims we've just quoted aren't all true aims — that only the last one, the new business objective, is specific enough to be called an aim. That assumes that an aim has got to be spelt out with figures and dates, which isn't necessarily so. It's really a word-problem — a question of the way managers understand the different terms they use in talking about the ideas that give them a sense of direction:

— **purpose** normally suggests a very broad kind of aim — the reason someone has for doing something. It's the answer to a question such as "why have such a department as this?" or "why does this job exist?" or "what's the point of this activity?"

— **aim** usually implies a particular direction in which things are to be moved. Often that is all it suggests, without any specific destination — as when a manager says he's aiming to improve the way something is done. But 'aim' does often get used in the sense of an aiming-point, some specific goal to be achieved — as a manager might say his aim is to complete a task by the end of this week.

— **objective, target** and **goal** all seem to be completely interchangeable. Some managers make subtle distinctions between them, but that's only a kind of private jargon. All three words mean an aiming-point — a situation specific enough to recognise when you've arrived there. Usually it's defined by figures and dates: the goal is to achieve a certain result by the end of the month; the target is to improve throughput by 10% within 6 months; the objective is to keep this monthly figure within ±4% of the amount set in the cash-flow forecast.

— **terms of reference** are aims for a committee investigating something, or for a project group brought together to solve a problem. They define the questions the committee or group are to try to answer (and so imply what questions are *not* to be considered).

The real distinction between different types of aim is in their *depth.* If you think of the operations going on in your section or department as a sea of activity and decision-making, aims are the various currents in the sea. Many are at the surface — the immediate purposes of the different activities, short-term objectives, specific targets. Others run deeper — longer-term aims and objectives, the underlying sense of purpose, the feelings about what's really important that are shared by all involved. Aims at the different depths are all necessary. Without the targets and objectives that give purpose to whatever they're doing day by day, week by week, month by month, people can't feel they're getting anywhere with them. But there isn't much point in getting there unless it contributes to deeper purposes, broader aims, longer-term goals.

Think of the way our personal aims for ourselves shape up — it's not so very different from the aims of organisations and of the groups inside them. At a surface level, we have reasons for the things we do, immediate goals for immediate actions. Often different aims are satisfied in one and the same activity: you want to meet your friends in the pub and you also want some exercise. The first aim decides the direction you go, the second persuades you to walk instead of taking the car. Or different activities might serve one and the same aim: you get exercise by walking and also by doing some gardening. But the point about aims like these is that they all lie close to the surface. They are immediate aims for a fairly immediate result.

Beneath them are deeper aims that aren't always so obvious. Go on questioning each reason a person comes up with for doing something — "yes, but *why* do you want to achieve that?" — and if you don't get a poke in the eye, you eventually reach a barrier of another sort. He can't explain any further. There comes a stage where most of us haven't analysed our own motives that far. You're trying to get back to a person's fundamental values, and they're rarely easy to put into words.

To illustrate how a person's aims connect with one another, imagine the ways different people might answer the question "Why are you reading this book?" There'll be 'surface' aims like these:

- "to see if it offers me any new insights into management."

194

- ''to find support for my existing management methods.''
- ''to learn any useful management techniques I can apply.''
- ''because it aroused my curiosity.''
- ''to occupy some idle time.''

Suppose you then ask each person about the aim he has given: ''and why d'you want to do *that*?'' He has a deeper aim below that one — an aim that motivates a lot of other things he does too:

- ''to broaden my understanding of what management is about.''
- ''to find ways to improve my management performance.
- ''to defend myself against some criticism I'm getting.''
- ''to prove my own thinking is better than other people's.''
- ''to justify to myself the way I'm spending my time.''

Question those in turn, and there are yet deeper aims:

- ''to develop whatever potential I've got to the furthest extent that I can.''
- ''to enable me to feel I'm doing a worthwhile job.''
- ''to help my organisation to be more effective.''
- ''to enhance my promotion prospects.''
- ''for the sake of an easy life.''

For different people, one or another of those aims might be the driving force.

Eventually these connect up with each person's deepest aims of all — his basic motivation in life itself. For one person it might be 'success', however he sees it: personal status and possessions perhaps, or simply being regarded as successful by others. For another person, the aim might be self-fulfilment: perhaps becoming very able at something, or taking pride in his creative achievements, or meeting and conquering difficult challenges. For yet another, the aim might be personal power. For another, the need to fulfil a duty to society. For another, simply the pursuit of personal pleasures.

The aims of groups and organisations work in much the same way. Near the surface are their immediate reasons for the things they do. Then there are their objectives for activities over the next few days or weeks — short-term so that people don't lose sight of them, and specific so that everyone is quite clear whether or not each objective has been achieved. They are the currents that keep the traffic of daily activities moving in the right directions. Beneath them are the longer-term aims for the months and years ahead, towards which the more immediate aims contribute. Their intended results lie too far into the future to be specified with the same precision, but that doesn't make them any the less important. They set bearings for all the more immediate objectives, create the sense of direction that's required to determine the kinds of shorter-term goals that are needed.

Then there are the most fundamental aims of all for organisations — their basic orientations, the emphasis that managers give to their underlying priorities. Is it the main point of their organisation to be a profit-machine? Or to serve the cause of technical excellence? Or to be sensitive to its market? Or to maintain its authority over the public? Such an aim amounts to the organisational articles of faith. It's often as difficult to pin down as the ultimate values of an individual. If you try to put it into words, they can only be crude approximations. Within the organisation, it's almost impossible for managers to conceive of it as being anything other than it is — anyone who thinks differently is either perverted or stupid. In fact, that is sometimes the best way to specify it: to try to produce a negative of it, to see who can commit the worst blasphemy against the organisation's creed. For Rolls Royce for instance it might have been: "So who cares if it's a crude bit of engineering? It's cheap and we can sell it at a huge profit." For a certain large hotel group which used to boast about its staff's attitudes to its guests, it was the attempt by the manager of a hotel that had become highly successful (and profitable) to reward his staff whose dedicated efforts had had much to do with the success. When he proposed a modest increase in their pay, his boss reacted in amazement: "are you *mad* George? D'you want to *give* money away?" That tells you a lot about the organisation's basic creed.

What all this is trying to suggest is that aim-setting isn't something a manager can do quickly, off-the-cuff — not if he wants to develop good aims for his operation. In fact it's not quite true to say you set an aim. More accurately, you realise what the aim ought to be. And the longer you can think it through, the better the aim you're likely to come up with. It's a mental process of trying to weave together three strands in your thinking about whatever operation you're concerned with:

1. What's actually happening in it now — the kinds of internal problem you see there, the strengths that are available to be build on.

2. What might happen in the future — the possibilities, the risks and dangers, the changes that might be forced on the operation by external events or trends.

3. Its fundamental purpose — what it's supposed to contribute, how that purpose might be better achieved, in what direction you ought to try to move things.

The mental process takes time. It's rather like cooking a meal. There's a natural cooking speed for a stew or a hot-pot. The slower it cooks, the better the result. The cook can avoid wasting time, but once he has done so he can't hasten the cooking speed any further without spoiling the final product. On the other hand if he uses the time available in the wrong way, even though there's ample time on the face of it, the meat still comes out inedible.

There *are* activities where faster does mean better, where working under pressure brings out the best. But it doesn't apply to the kind of brain-work involved in thinking out your aims and objectives, particularly the longer-term ones. You need time to think through the information you've got; time to discuss ideas with others — colleagues, subordinates, bosses; time to figure out just what the problems are. There's even value in making fresh starts after interruptions to your train of thought, the effect a break and then a resumption has in bringing in new ideas, different ways of looking at the whole question. It's the same as when you leave a crossword puzzle half-finished: coming back to it in the morning, you quickly solve clues that were impossibly elusive the night before.

Too often, managers won't accept that their definitions of aims (or failures to define them) cause any difficulties in the operations they're running. Faced with a job that needs to be tackled but where it's not easy to define an objective, they have two alternative approaches. One manager will confidently expect things "to firm up soon, when we'll be able to specify our objectives" — and continues to put off making a start. Another will instantly snatch out of the air a briefly-stated aim that is so loose his staff have actually to work out their terms of reference for themselves. Neither end of the scale is very satisfactory.

What you have to accept is that aims often have to be allowed to clarify themselves as the work to achieve them gets under way. You begin by 'pencilling in' what seems to be a reasonable aim to get started with. But during the groundwork in the early stages of the task or project, you are looking to sharpen or re-shape the aim, possibly even re-think it totally, as you discover more about what is involved. It's not an easy method of aim-setting to manage. Before the action begins, there's often a demand to know exactly what is the intended result, how long will it take, what will it cost. But managers really have to stop letting the world think it's possible for them to work out such things with any precision right at the start. More honesty would be better management.

The danger of fixing too early on a misconceived aim is the effects in misdirecting people's efforts. They will tend to regard it as a rigid rule rather than as a guide to intelligent action, and will continue to pursue it even when it has become abundantly clear that the aim needs to be changed. Committees' terms of reference are a common example: so often, the need to rewrite them becomes patently obvious during the first couple of meetings. Yet chairmen who are fully aware of the fact will still rule that the committee has to do the best it can with the terms of reference it has been given, and not one dissenting voice will be raised. It is almost as though the honour of the committee depends on its continuing with the given purpose simply because it has been given, never mind how ridiculous it turns out to be. It's traditionally considered a sign of weaknes to complain about the terms of reference.

By contrast, there was this project set up in a big organisation that was using a computer model to evaluate the needs to invest in new plant. The project was to test the model's validity: were its evaluations accurate enough to continue using it? It didn't take long for the project team to realise they'd been given the wrong question to answer. The model's validity wasn't the issue. The real question was: did the model provide a better guide for investment decisions than simple methods? In this case the project aim *was* revised. The team eventually reached their conclusion: no, the simple methods were just as good as the model — and far cheaper and quicker into the bargain. Had they continued with their original question, the organisation might still have been using the computer model. It *was* perfectly valid, even though quite unnecessary.

In setting aims for projects and working parties and all kinds of one-off tasks, what is often needed is a commitment to review the initial idea at a later stage. Like any other sort of decision, an aim is never totally right — and just possibly might be totally wrong. But in one important way, it *is* different from many other decisions: an aim can be changed (or at least adjusted) *after* you've started moving in that direction, whereas something you've decided to do, once done can't be undone. Naturally you don't want to change it without good reason. With many aims, the pay-off comes from persistence in pursuing them in the face of difficulties — you don't give up when the going gets tough. But that's not true of an aim that's quite clearly wrong. No doubt, getting course corrections accepted by others does take some effort, but not too much if you've taken care to write into your first draft of the aim the intention to reconsider it at a given point when you can reasonably expect the problems and possibilities to be better understood. Normally you'd be able to do this fairly early in the whole exercise before much time and effort has been wasted in a wrong direction.

So what does aim-setting mean in practice for you as a manager? Try answering these questions about the way you actually do it:

## 1. Do you *have* aims for your operation?

Real aims, that is, not like those nondescript things we illustrated earlier — achieving superiors' targets, seeing people do as they're supposed to, administering things efficiently and so on. Be honest. Have you really worked out your ideas about the direction in which you're trying to steer your operation and your people? Or do you let things take their course and simply react to each problem as it emerges? If you're the sort of manager who *makes* things happen, then you'll have ideas about such things as these:

- You'll have thought about the purpose of the various activities you and your people are engaged on. You'll have found an explanation for yourself of what the whole operation you run is there for.
- You'll have tried to establish what are the reasons for the policies and systems you operate.
- You'll have in mind the results you're trying to get achieved through all the work you're responsible for. What do you want it to accomplish in the next, say, six months or a year that will be different from the last?
- You'll know what to concentrate on to achieve those results, what's important about the work that goes into producing them.
- You'll look for ways of doing things better. You'll have aims to improve specific aspects of the operation you run.
- Your aims will take account of external problems you can foresee. You'll try to use to advantage any opportunities you expect to open up.

If you feel tempted to argue that your superiors work out all these things so there's no point in your duplicating what they're doing, do they really? Haven't you got any ideas of your own? Shouldn't you be able to come up with better focussed, more practical aims than other people who aren't so directly involved in the work — even if they *are* senior to you? What have you done to persuade your boss to listen to your ideas?

## 2. Are your aims clear?

Personal aims usually don't need to be explicitly stated. For the individual, the question is simply whether he himself knows what he's about. A manager's aims are different. They have to be clear not only to the manager who developed them but also to a lot of other people besides. They've got to be understood by his superiors, in case his aims don't fit in with their broader purposes; by his colleagues, to sort out problems of conflict between his aims and theirs; by his subordinates particularly, because they'll be involved in achieving the aims and need to harmonise their own goals with them. Managerial aims have to be spelt out in *words*.

For many aims — those that take the form of objectives, targets and goals — words aren't enough by themselves. *Figures* are needed too: how much by when? At what cost over how long? An objective that says something like "we want to reduce our spending somehow" is pointless. Precisely what kinds of spending do we intend to reduce? By how much? How quickly? You have to specify quantities, frequencies, amounts, timings, dates so that everyone concerned can measure progress towards the objective and will know whether or not it has been achieved. If it *isn't* achieved, there may well be *other* objectives that have to be adjusted to compensate. Precise figures are needed in most short-term operational goals, and in almost any kind of cost or revenue target. Money generally doesn't mean very much unless it's counted out.

But there are other aims that you can't actually pin down with figures — particularly aims to do with the *quality* of results or with *people's* performance or their management. Try to convert that sort of aim into a numbers game and you divert people's attention from the main point.

For instance, suppose you are aiming to improve the quality of your area's output in some way. Output quality, you reckon, is reflected in the frequency of complaints you get from those receiving the output — although this isn't a totally foolproof indicator (no indicator ever is). If the number of complaints falls, probably quality is improving. So you specify the level you want to see complaints reduced to. Have you stated an aim? No, it's a standard — a way of estimating the quality being provided. *Aims and standards are two different things.* It's a common weakness of unthinking managements to get them confused. Your aim is still to improve the quality: don't start letting your people think it's simply to reduce the number of complaints, or some smart operator will discover a way of doing that without doing anything to raise the output quality.

Long-term, strategic aims can hardly ever be quantified in any meaningful way. Nor do they need to be. The point of having them isn't to be able to measure progress or to know when they're achieved. It is to create a sense of direction for the medium and short-term aims that *can* be specified that way. Indeed, the important thing about really long-term aims might be more to do with keeping your options open than with specifying destinations. The practical possibilities are too uncertain that far in advance. So you set up your aims into the further future as a check on your more immediate goals: they exist to help you avoid sacrificing long-term opportunities for the sake of short-term and short-lived advantages.

This means of course that strategic aims are pointless by themselves. They've got to connect with the practical goals on which managers and their people are actually operating *now*. An aim that is entirely divorced from current actions, that has absolutely no influence over managers' decisions today, is hardly an aim at all — more a pious hope. Unless a long-term aim is already being implemented through your short-term goals, forget it.

### 3. Are your aims realistic?

Unrealistic aims come in two varieties. One is the aim that simply cannot be achieved, given the circumstances and the people who are supposed to make it work. Maybe it would be achievable in a different situation or with larger resources or with greater ability or commitment. But as things are, it's not an aim. It's an ideal.

There was this newly-appointed sales manager who thought to make his presence felt by shocking his complacent sales force out of their lazy lives. He started setting the monthly sales targets by the top performance anyone in the team had achieved in the same month last year. The new targets for everyone were to match that performance. They took the required results from down here to 'way over everyone's head. Of course, within the first month they had become a joke throughout the organisation. History doesn't record what happened to the manager, but a promotion wasn't the likely outcome.

But if over-high aims are self-defeating, the other sort of unrealistic aim has nothing to defeat. It's the aim that will be achieved anyway — the aim that is too low, that'll be secured perfectly easily by the time-honoured process of letting matters take their own course. It's unrealistic because it doesn't take a reasonable view of what *could* be achieved with a bit of effort and imagination. In fact it isn't an aim at all. It's a forecast of minimal results.

Unrealistic aims of both varieties come about when managers don't try to *visualise* what their aims will mean in practical terms. They don't imagine future possibilities and probabilities. Instead they suppose the future will be a replay of their records and memories of what's already happened, or they play the game of 'let's pretend': let's pretend the equipment will never break down. Let's pretend we aren't suffering from those problems that persist in our operation. Let's pretend the jobs we'll be doing will contain no unexpected difficulties. Let's pretend our people are totally incapable of human error. It's no argument to say that an aim can't take account of such things because they're unpredictable. That's your job as a manager — to make your own judgements of what sort of allowances should be made for them in aim-setting. For instance:

— if you must set targets on the basis of last year's

results, at least try to look forward at what percentage plus or minus it's reasonable to expect — bearing in mind the way your forecasts suggest things are moving for next year. The sales target that's set at a rule-of-thumb 15% (or whatever) on top of last year's figure often has its most marked consequence in the withered morale of the sales force.

— when you're setting aims for volumes and timings of future workloads, don't be pressured into filling the available capacity 100%. Allow for the need to 'shape' the forward work programmes so there's slack time left in the system. It's there as recovery-time for when things go adrift. With experience you should learn how much time needs to be left unallocated.

The most consistent mistakes in setting objectives and targets are in calculating what it's possible to get done in a given time. If you under-estimate how long some work will take to complete, the consequences are often expensive problems of coordination. There's a domino effect. *This* work late means delays in all those *other* jobs whose time-targets have been set on the assumption that your objective for the work was a realistic one. And those delays are going to cause even bigger headaches further down the line...

Despite the risks, many managers deliberately persist in setting time deadlines that turn tasks and projects into rush-jobs, presumably on the argument that the greater the pressure, the better do people respond. With some kinds of work there may be some truth in this. But it is difficult to avoid the suspicion that often the argument has about as much validity as the claim that people drive better after a drink or two. They only *feel* better about the way they drive.

It's often assumed that almost any job can be done faster or slower, and that the only thing that is affected is the cost. In research and development, for instance, some managers consider that a project can be performed at a number of different rates, each consistent with the research strategy but requiring a different budget. Time and again, this idea has been demonstrated to be untrue. Not only do the costs go up as the pace is forced, but also the quality of the research output goes down. With brain-work, crash projects produce worse answers. If there is a fixed quantity of resources — a given level of funding, say, to solve a problem — then fewer people working for longer will always be more productive than more people working faster.

## 4. Do your aims sort out your priorities?

Aim-setting isn't much use unless it helps you and your people make better judgements in the decision-making you all have to do. Out of the hundred-and-one things you could be trying to attend to, which particular ones are the most important to focus attention on? And how do you balance your attention *between* them?

For instance, suppose that aims have been set for a project to build a new production unit: the unit is to be completed within a specified cost and time, and is to produce a specified quality of product at a specified rate within specified operating costs. As an aim, that is almost completely useless. It puts together five objectives that all affect each other — they are interdependent variables — but doesn't say how they're to be *balanced*. When problems crop up that put the completion-date at risk (and if the aim doesn't take account of that near-certainty, it's *totally* useless), what is the important thing? It might be possible to recover the time loss by spending more money; on the other hand, reducing some of the perfomance criteria of the finished plant may enable other parts of the work to be speeded up without any over-spending at all. It's essential to know the order of the priorities: is time more crucial than cost, or is it the other way about? And how is the operating economy and capacity of the eventual plant to be reckoned against them?

Nor is it a simple question of saying "this is priority number one, this is number two..." and so on. That may be the order in one set of circumstances, but suppose circumstances change? Perhaps you say that time is the key priority, and that costs must be increased beyond target if necessary to recover any time-slippage. Yes, but how far can costs exceed budget in that situation before it becomes more important to hold *them* down than to rescue any more of the time-slippage? These are the kinds of questions that objectives ought to help sort out. If they don't do that, they haven't really been thought through.

Whatever sort of operation you run, you'll inevitably have conflicts to resolve in the aims you set. Often there'll be difficulties in satisfying the various interests of other areas whose work interlocks with yours or is somehow affected by what you're doing on your patch. Imagine for instance you're running a purchasing section in a manufacturing outfit. Think of the other departments who are affected by the purchasing decisions you and your staff are taking — whom you decide to place orders with, how you specify what they're to supply, the terms and conditions you negotiate with them... What might other departments' interests be in the ways you take those decisions?

- Manufacturing wants an assured supply to prevent any hold-ups in production work-flows.
- Finance wants low cost, good discounts, long credit.
- Sales want a quality that will appeal to customers.
- Product Design wants a range that will offer scope to develop new versions of existing products.

They *can't* all be satisfied equally. So you have to set purchasing aims that create the best balance you can manage.

Aim-setting is a very misunderstood aspect of the management job. The phrase 'Management by Objectives' became something of a fad in the 1960s and a lot of consultancy reputations were made on schemes to 'install MbO' in different organisations. Quite apart from the question of whether objectives *can* be 'installed' like mains drainage, the fact that they had become a fashion made many managements doubt whether objectives were relevant to their organisations — which is roughly equivalent to questioning whether destinations are relevant to transport systems.

Without aims that they have developed for themselves, managers can't *manage* anything in the proper sense of the word. They cannot truly use their own judgement to shape the operations they are supposed to be responsible for. They merely calculate how best to obey the commands and policies of their superiors. To have an aim implies commitment. Ultimately it is a self-directing mechanism in a human mind. Managers need that sort of motivation.

But there's more than this to aims. Besides the personal motivation they provide, they also satisfy a broader requirement in an organisation. Aims pull management groups and work-force units into teams — *if* they are developed in the right way within each group, through discussion, mutual understanding and positive leadership. If you are truly a leader, your aims aren't aims for you alone. All the people who report to you have a stake in them too, have helped you to shape them, are taking part in refining and reshaping them when necessary. Aims and objectives aren't managers' personal property. They belong to teams.

That was the real message of Management by Objectives that got lost underneath all the clever systems, the involved paperwork, the pressuring of individuals that were applied in the name of MbO. The manager who has aims for himself and his people possesses one of the key qualifications for leadership. The manager who has no aims, or whose aims concern solely his own activities, lacks that qualification. MbO is the only kind of leadership that's available to managers at any level.

## C. Management by Anticipation

There are two broad classes of management failure: failures of intention and failures of execution. The first are often the fault of managers who have weaknesses in the forecasting and aim-setting department. The second are the outcome of bad detailed planning — and they're the more common variety. Managers are more frequently guilty of ruining sensible strategies by sloppy tactics than of wasting excellent execution trying to accomplish something that's inherently absurd.

The difference between good and bad planning is often in the manager's attitude to the problems, errors and unknowns that could de-rail his plans. Bad planning is the sort that assumes you can deal with problems only in arrears. Good planning tries to prevent the problems from cropping up in the first place — and there's often more scope for that than managers realise. The time you want to find out about mistakes is before they're made. But neither controls nor forecasts can do that: controls don't pre-date the action, and forecasts can't give you that kind of information. Proper management of the planning process *can* alert you to potential errors and inefficiencies before they've had time to cause waste and confusion.

Look at what happens. In a factory the production controller forecasts the requirements for materials and orders them from the stores. As production proceeds, his controls collect evidence of the amount of waiting time caused by material shortages. He analyses this information to find the proportion it represents of total production hours, and compares it with his previous records to see if waiting time is increasing or reducing. Is the production controller really managing the problem? Not a bit of it. The forecasts don't prevent the shortages, and the controls don't reduce the time-wasting.

Move over to the sales department. The sales manager looks at his annual sales objectives and sets the monthly targets for his sales force. The salesmen go around their territories making sales calls and sending in their visit reports to tell him where they've been and what business they've got. The information is carefully collated and compared with the targets. Is the sales manager really managing the work of the sales force? Not on your life. If the customers visited aren't likely to provide the targetted sales, the reports won't change the fact. And if a proportion of the sales are to bad payers and poor credit risks, the business is of dubious value to the firm.

Or consider almost anyone who's been asked by his boss to write a report for more senior management. He drafts the report and then passes it to his boss, who goes through it checking it and rewriting large sections because he reckons the content and emphasis is wrong. Is the boss really managing the report-writing task? No — he's actually doing a large part of it himself. Into the bargain, he's convincing his report-writing subordinate there's no point in trying to make his future reports even half-decent, because whatever he writes the boss will rewrite. The right time for action is before wrong decisions are implemented.

Now replay those three situations.

The production controller gets the supervisors regularly to look ahead to see whether every worker has enough work to do for at least the next few hours. Before shortages create waiting time, he hears about them and either pushes the stores to get their finger out or instructs the supervisors to move the men to other tasks. He *anticipates* the problem — meaning he does something about it ahead of time.

The sales manager asks his salesmen to keep him supplied

with their visit plans for the next month, updated weekly perhaps. If he can see that a plan isn't likely to provide the required business, he suggests changing ports of call or trying other ideas he has. He also checks the plans against Credit Control's lists of outstanding accounts. If visits to those customers are planned, he makes sure the salesman knows that cheques have to be collected before accepting further orders. He *anticipates* the problem.

The report-writer is asked by his boss to map out brief notes on how he intends to arrange his report. Before it's drafted the boss checks over the notes with his subordinate and suggests where different questions might be answered or which points will need careful treatment. As far as possible he tries to prevent the *need* for later rewriting. He *anticipates* the problem. Do you get the idea?

Notice who's doing the planning in each case. It isn't actually the production controller or the sales manager or the report-writer's boss. They're each getting their *subordinates* to think out what they intend doing or what needs to be done — because their staff are the people who are standing closer to the situation, who should have the most practical ideas, who have in any case to put the plans into action. In this sort of approach, the manager's skill is to be able to look at a plan and visualise how it will work out in practice. It demands a bit of imagination. That's an ability that some managers declare they haven't got by their comments on any plans they're shown. Either the changes they suggest are badly judged and make the plan worse, not better, or they don't know what to think: "er, well I think it looks all right — er, we'll just have to see how it works out, won't we?"

But more commonly, what prevents managers from managing by anticipation isn't that it's difficult or that they're not clever enough to do it. It's that all their habits run counter to the idea. If a job over-runs or last month's target wasn't achieved or an item on the budget was overspent, the inevitable question is "why?" Managers are conditioned to demand information about the past. Conceivably the answers they get could have value in the future, but it's likely to be the long-term future — in lessons that can be learned, in mistakes that can be avoided if anything similar turns up again. The immediate need is better served by another type of question: "what could make the *current* job overrun?" "What could prevent our target for *next* month from being achieved?" "What could cause *this* quarter's budget to be overspent?" In other words, the question tries to control a future problem rather than prompting excuses for a past failure.

Nor is aim-setting enough to reveal the potential snags. You have to think through *what has to be done* to achieve your goals and targets, including taking account of existing difficulties that still haven't been fully solved. For a huge number of managers, one of their commonest failings is to be slipshod about doing this. They neglect to think in enough detail of each piece of the action that'll be required to bring about the future situation or result they intend. Without that detailed thinking it's impossible to spot the things that could go wrong, let alone decide how to pre-empt the problems. If you want to find out whether a manager is thinking ahead in enough detail for proper Management by Anticipation, ask him about his contingency plans — what possible snags he has foreseen and what he intends doing if they seem likely to cause trouble. If he doesn't have an answer, or if his answer is vague, his planning is probably defective.

Many managers' planning is all done in their heads. At least, that's where they claim to do it — if they do it at all. They hardly ever use even the proverbial back of a used envelope. However often their memories prove unreliable, however big the difficulties caused by obvious points they've missed, they still dodge the act of writing things down. It's the typical failure of the 'action-man' type of manager that he avoids that particular discipline, even if it is of the simplest kind.

There is an enormous range of possible methods of planning. Here are a few of the more important ones:

## 1. Thinking ahead

A lot of the planning that managers need to do doesn't actually require pen and paper. The first rule is Stop and Think: ''what's really happening here?''... ''what alternatives have I got?''... ''what would be the outcome of doing this rather than that?''... ''what ought I to be doing at the moment?''... ''what if I leave that task until tomorrow?''...

Planning is a *thinking* reaction to situations and events in an attempt to control their consequences. It's a reaction that isn't available to the manager who gets aggressive when things don't go his way, who becomes angry at criticisms or imagined slights, who responds to a request to get something done by attacking the requester: ''you must be joking. Can't you see I've got enough to do as it is?'' Nor is it available to the manager who is too submissive, too anxious to please: ''well I don't really have any time to spare, but I suppose I could let something else go if you insist.'' Managers like that are non-planners. They try to deal with every situation as it arises, and waste time and effort in an environment of half-finished tasks and disorganised urgency.

If you think ahead, you deal with the same problem in a more matter-of-fact way: "I can't do that at the moment, but I understand why it needs to be done. Let's see what the alternatives are..." If there's a demand for a decision you're less likely to plunge for a snap answer: "I need to think about that.

Can I let you have my decision later on?" You don't attack others' rights like the aggressive manager, nor do you let your own rights be trampled on — the undoing of the weak manager. You are *assertive* about what seems to you the sensible thing to do in the situation.

## 2. The notebook
You know how quickly you can forget an idea you've just had? Five minutes later you can remember only that you've had it — not what it was. The notebook is an insurance against such lapse of memory — a small pocket-book for jotting things down as you think of them:

- thoughts that occur to you for possible action.
- bits of information people mention in conversation.
- requests made to you.
- agreements you've made with others during discussions.
- reminders of things you want to look into.
- points you observe that need attention.

— instructions you've given that will require progress checks later.

Apart from dating your notes, you're not likely to be able to organise those jottings of course. They're unsorted. Some may not turn out to be very important — but you have to be sure that no pearls slip your mind. Many of them might become inputs to your other planning techniques that *are* rather more organised — do-lists or the diary perhaps.

To be useful, you keep the note-book with you constantly wherever you go so that you're not reduced to making notes on scrappy bits of paper that get lost. It has to become a regular managerial habit to pull out the note-book and scribble a reminder to yourself in it.

### 3. Do-lists

The shopping-list technique for short-term planning. It's a plain sheet of paper listing the things you have to deal with over the next day or two. Most of the items will be fairly quick tasks.

— letters or memos to write.
— telephone calls to make.
— visits or meetings to arrange.
— points to take up with people.
— things to check up on.
— small difficulties to resolve.
— information to get.
— decisions about future, bigger tasks etc.

You make out the list first thing in the morning — or even last thing before you leave work the previous day. Further items are added as they arise during the day or as you think of them...

Each item is crossed off the list as it's dealt with. Next day you transfer the outstanding items to a new list and start again.

Do-lists are a basic method of planning your time. Besides ensuring that small things don't get forgotten, they can also make it easier to identify your immediate priorities and so to organise your time more effectively. Having made the list, you can then weigh up the relative urgency and importance of each task and star those items that *must* be done today. You can also sequence the tasks in a time-effective way, putting together things that should be done together (e.g. several phone calls to make or letters to write). You can even sort out suitable timings with other people for things listed that they'll also be involved in — making the best use of both your time and theirs.

In one organisation each supervisor is encouraged to sit down towards the end of each day with pencil and paper to plan his next day's activities. Some have even developed their own check lists of regular activities and operations. They tick off the things that they can expect to go according to plan, and so highlight the possible trouble-spots to concentrate on during the following day — or to refer to their bosses if they cannot sort them out themselves. That way everyone is helped to see where problems can be prevented by early action, which is what Management by Anticipation is all about.

## 4. The diary

Surprisingly, this is a planning technique that is very under-used by many managers — the desk diary, or the pocket diary if your job keeps you on the move. Not that managers don't use the diary, but many don't use it all that effectively. It has one obvious purpose and another less obvious but equally important:

> — the obvious purpose is to note future DATES: appointments, bring-forward dates for items to be followed up, times when you will be away on visits or at meetings.
> — the less obvious purpose is to set aside PERIODS in the future for non-urgent but important large-scale tasks. These periods then become commitments that you try to keep clear of any avoidable interruptions.

Do-lists and the diary can be worked together. As a date becomes current in the diary, it is transferred to the do-list for that day — ensuring that it's properly fitted in with the other tasks on the do-list. In any case make a habit of *checking the diary daily,* preferably first thing. What's the point of religiously recording your future dates if you don't look to see when they've arrived?

## 5. Action plans

This is the basic method for planning a project (or any large task) where at the start you can't be sure what will be involved altogether. Properly done, it's a problem-prevention technique. It aims to get something achieved with the fewest possible hitches or unforeseen difficulties cropping up during the action.

That kind of action plan needs to be worked out systematically:

Step 1:     STATE THE AIM. However obvious it seems to be, write it down. But don't allow your thinking to become fixated on the first aim you come up with. You'll probably need to reconsider it later when you've thought through the problem. Here it's an initial idea of what you're trying to accomplish that you pencil in to orientate your thinking.

Step 2:     WHAT'S THE PROBLEM? In this sense, the 'problem' is the sum of the differences between where you are at the moment and where you're trying to get to. Note down all the facts of the present situation that might have a bearing on what you're trying to do. If there are things that could be relevant where you don't actually have information, define the *questions* you want to try to get answered. Include notes on any difficulties you can foresee:

- practical obstacles.
- organisational constraints.
- possible resistance from people.
- financial limitations.
- the risks of side-effects etc.

Think too of any future opportunities that could be used to clear the path. Are things likely to happen that could reduce any resistance you're likely to meet? Could imminent events make what you're trying to achieve more attractive to others involved — or less attractive? *Don't start to fix any solutions in your mind until you're sure you understand the problem.*

Now RECONSIDER YOUR AIM. Can you define it more precisely? Improve on it? Make it more practicable? Should you scrap the whole idea and start again on a different tack?

Step 3:     WHAT HAS TO BE DONE? Note down all the actions required to achieve the aim from the starting position you've now mapped out. Don't try to organise them yet. Just think around all the needs to see what has to be put into the pot. And remember the needs to involve others and explain things to them. The plan's success may depend on whether you're able to get them to go along with it.

Step 4:    MAKE THE PLAN. Decide where to begin, and list the actions in time-sequence. Against each one, note who will be involved and set a deadline for its completion. Even if some of the deadlines have to be somewhat notional, it's worth having them as aiming-points to work towards.

If the different actions have complicated inter-relationships, you might well consider using a charting technique to work out their arrangement and timings (perhaps one of the techniques we're coming to in a moment).

Step 5:    PREPARE FOR CONTINGENCIES. No plan ever works out exactly as intended. But many of the practical snags that disrupt it might have been obvious from the start if the manager had thought it through. Good planning includes forethought for the problems that could upset its implementation — Management by Anticipation again.

Consider where things could go wrong: accidents that could increase costs or require an unexpected amount of effort, delays that could throw interlocking activities out of gear, side-effects that could create major difficulties, events that could overtake the plan. Decide what you could do about the most likely or most serious dangers. What precautions should be included in the plan? Where should you monitor progress? What scope is there for adjusting the timing or sequence of tasks on the run? Where are contingency plans needed for serious breakdowns? What could be rescued if the plan suffers a total derailment?

All of this may sound vastly over-complicated for the activities you manage. Perhaps it is, for regular activities or simple projects. But the basic principles still apply:

— be clear about what you're trying to achieve.
— get a good understanding of the problems.
— make sure the planned action is adequate for the circumstances.
— anticipate difficulties.

## 6. Task/time charts

A technique for visualising how tasks can be fitted into time-periods. The tasks might be different elements of a project, or they may be different activities to be done in your neck of the woods. What the technique assumes is that all the tasks are known beforehand, and that it's possible to estimate reasonably accurately the time needed for each one. Charting is particularly useful when the tasks are inter-related and there are too many of them to see from a simple list how their timings can best be fitted together.

The chart is a grid that plots the tasks against time-periods (days, weeks or whatever). For instance:

| Tasks | Week 1 | | | | | Week 2 | | | | | Week 3 | | | | |
|---|---|---|---|---|---|---|---|---|---|---|---|---|---|---|---|
| | 1 | 2 | 3 | 4 | 5 | 1 | 2 | 3 | 4 | 5 | 1 | 2 | 3 | 4 | 5 |
| Task A | ░ | ░ | ░ | ░ | | | | | | | | | | | |
| Task B | ░ | | | | | ▥ | | | | | ░ | | | | |
| Task C | | ░ | ░ | ░ | ░ | | | | | | | | | | |
| Task D | | | | | | ░ | ░ | ░ | ░ | | | | | | |
| Task E | | | | | | | | | | | | | ░ | ░ | ░ |

Blocking in the boxes like this is the simplest way of using the chart. Alternatively you might plot the number of hours required or the number of staff needed day by day... There are many possibilities. Such charts are often called Gantt Charts after the man who first developed the idea of using them, Henry Gantt.

The point of charting is that it's often easier to plan when you can create a visual pattern to see what you're doing. The chart also makes it easier to discuss the plan with others who'll be involved, to try out the effects of any changes they suggest, and to ensure that everyone understands what ought to happen when. As the plan is implemented, a further advantage is that the chart makes progress easier to monitor. If tasks are delayed or over-run, you can quickly see the consequences for the rest of the plan and adjust its timings to suit.

## 7. Resource/time charts

A variation on task/time charting. Its main use is when the problem is how to match demands to a particular physical resource, for instance:
— members of staff.

— items of equipment (machines, vehicles etc.).
— units of accommodation.

Again it uses a grid, but here it's one that sets units of the resource against the time-periods. It shows when each unit is available or is booked for use.

Suppose you manage staff who work on assignments and want a quick method of checking where your people are and who is free to take on further assignments. You might operate a chart like this to show who's working when on assignments A, B, C and so on.

| Staff | Weeks | | | | | | | |
|-------|---|---|---|---|---|---|---|---|
| | 1 | 2 | 3 | 4 | 5 | 6 | 7 | |
| T. Jones | | ←──(A)──→ | | | ←──(B)──→ | | | |
| R. Brown | ←(C)→ | | ←(A)→ | | | ←──(D)── | ---- | |
| P. Smith | | ←──(B)──→ | | | | | | |
| J. Robinson | ←(C)→ | | | | ←──(B)──→ | | | |

You can read information from the visual pattern that you can't get from a series of lists — spotting quickly, for instance, which staff are working together on the different assignments over what periods.

Broadly speaking, there are two different purposes that resource/time charting can serve:
   — to plan for demands that are all known at the start of the total period covered by the chart. The chart is prepared as a fixed arrangement that, barring accidents, you don't expect to change during the period. You use it as a means of information and control (e.g. a staff rota — who's on duty, when).
   — To plan for demands that will build up progressively during the period. The charting is a continual 'on-line' process, developing from day to day as the period runs its course. You use the chart as a tool for decision-making (e.g. a car-hire booking chart — which cars are available, when).

Resource/time charting is a very common planning technique. It has a huge variety of uses: machine-utilisation charts in a workshop, room-allocation boards in a training centre, year-planners for staff leave...

## 8. Network diagrams

A technique for planning a large-scale project. Like task/time charting it creates a visual pattern of the tasks and time-periods involved. Unlike the simple chart, it shows how the tasks relate to one another — a big advantage with large and complicated programmes of project-work.

Suppose you have a project to plan that involves a lot of different tasks (say twenty or more) which all affect each other in various ways. Some can be done at the same time. Many have to be done in sequence: one task can't begin until another is complete. So it's difficult for you to work out the best arrangement for the timings of the various tasks one against another. Yet those time-relationships are absolutely crucial to the project's success — get them wrong and the result could be missed deadlines, wasted resources, excessive costs. The trouble is you don't know for which tasks the timings are most critical.

A task/time chart can't help you much in that situation. You could draw one up, right enough. But you wouldn't be able to see from it how all the tasks linked together and so work out the best and most efficient way of sequencing them. This is where a network diagram is just about the only way you *can* work things out. It will enable you to find which particular sequence of inter-linked tasks is the most crucial for the whole project's timing. This sequence of tasks is known as the 'critical path' for the project. The network diagramming technique is often called Critical Path Analysis (or CPA) for this reason.

Before the diagram can be prepared, you have to list all the tasks in the project and calculate how long each one will take. Defining the tasks isn't as straightforward as it sounds. You can over-detail them, making the separate pieces of activity too small and so getting too many of them to work into an effective plan. More commonly, managers don't detail them enough. Their plans bunch together what should be treated as several different tasks and so make it impossible to plan the links between their over-sized lumps of action. It also becomes difficult to calculate the duration of the tasks with any reasonable accuracy.

Once all the tasks and their durations are listed, the next

thing is to identify the starter task (or tasks): which tasks don't depend on any other tasks being completed first? All the rest of the tasks have the follow these — and many won't be able to start until yet *other* tasks are finished. You have to work out all these task relationships, or 'dependencies' as they are called.

The diagram is then built up, starting with the preliminary tasks. It uses two basic symbols:

> a circle represents an 'event' — a point in time when one or more tasks have been completed and others can therefore begin.

> an arrow represents an 'activity' — a task in progress. It runs from one 'event' circle to another; since it shows the passage of time its direction is important — it is an *arrow,* not merely a line.

To show how a diagram works, take a simple example. Suppose we have a project — let's say the outfitting of a building as an assembly plant. There are five activities that will have these durations:

| | |
|---|---|
| — plumbing | 3 days |
| — electrical work | 3 days |
| — partitioning | 2 days |
| — installing assembly equipment | 5 days |
| — painting | 4 days |

This is the network diagram drawn up for the project:

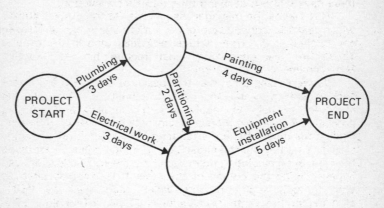

You'll notice the lengths of the arrows have nothing to do with the durations of the activities. All the diagram is concerned with is the *dependencies* between the activities:

218

- plumbing and electrical work don't depend on any other activities, and they are independent of each other too. Both can begin as soon as the project starts.
- neither partitioning nor painting can begin until plumbing is completed. But they themselves are independent of each other.
- equipment installation can't begin until both electrical work and partitioning are completed.
- painting and equipment installation are independent of each other. But the project isn't finished until both are completed.

Taking their *durations* into account, you can also see which activities govern the length of the project as a whole. You add up the timings on every sequence of activities to find which sequence gives you the longest total time. In this case it is:

- plumbing
- partitioning
- equipment installation

Done in the necessary sequence, they can't be completed in under ten days. They form the Critical Path and are identified by heavy lines in the diagram (a common way of indicating them). If any of those three over-runs, the project is bound to take longer. The other two activities each has a 'float' of time: electrical work can over-run by up to two days and painting by as much as three days without delaying the project's completion.

This means the manager responsible for the project knows which tasks to concentrate on. It's more important to foresee any hitches in the three critical activities than in the others. Those are the ones that most require him to practice Management by Anticipation.

Network diagrams are the basis of a variety of more sophisticated planning and control techniques. Many use the computer to help in resolving very complex programming problems. A really big project can include hundreds of activities. Finding the most efficient arrangement of all their relationships would be far beyond the capacities of human brains — let alone the work of recalculating them each time the inevitable slippages happen during the course of the project. It becomes possible only through such computer-based techniques as PERT, standing for 'Programme Evaluation and Review Technique'. But however sophisticated these approaches are, they have all grown out of the simple principles of network diagramming.

# Getting things done

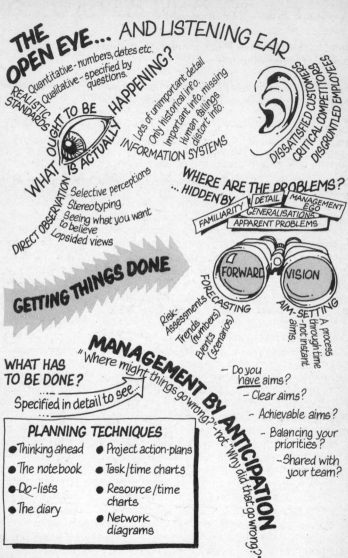

## THE OPEN EYE... AND LISTENING EAR

Quantitative - numbers, dates etc.
Qualitative - specified by questions.

REALISTIC STANDARDS

WHAT OUGHT TO BE HAPPENING?

WHAT IS ACTUALLY HAPPENING?

Lots of unimportant detail
Only historical info. missing
Important info.
Human failings distort info.

INFORMATION SYSTEMS

DISSATISFIED CUSTOMERS
CRITICAL COMPETITORS
DISGRUNTLED EMPLOYEES

DIRECT OBSERVATION
Selective perceptions
Stereotyping
Seeing what you want to believe
Lopsided views

### WHERE ARE THE PROBLEMS?
... HIDDEN BY

FAMILIARITY | DETAIL | MANAGEMENT EGO
GENERALISATIONS
APPARENT PROBLEMS

FORWARD VISION

FORECASTING
Risk-Assessments
Trends (numbers)
Events (scenarios)

AIM-SETTING
A process through time - not instant aims.

**GETTING THINGS DONE**

## MANAGEMENT BY ANTICIPATION
"Where might things go wrong?" - not "Why did that go wrong?"

### WHAT HAS TO BE DONE?
.... Specified in detail to see ...

– Do you have aims?
  – Clear aims?
  – Achievable aims?
  – Balancing your priorities?
  – Shared with your team?

### PLANNING TECHNIQUES
- Thinking ahead
- The notebook
- Do-lists
- The diary
- Project action-plans
- Task/time charts
- Resource/time charts
- Network diagrams

# WHAT IS A MANAGER?

The first of the Effective Management Skills books, *What is a Manager?* answers that question.

Even at a fairly junior level in an organisation you may be responsible for staff and projects and thus, a manager.

It also tells you who is not a manager. Once defined, the book helps the manager to develop essential management skills: organisation, delegation, innovative thinking.

All this written in a bright and accessible style, wittily illustrated by Paula Youens' cartoons.

# MANAGING PEOPLE

Managing People is one of the books in the Effective Management Skills series. This book gives useful and detailed advice on how to get the most out of your staff. How to make sure that they get the most out of their job. How to chair a meeting with greatest effect. How to hold an interview.

And other information you will need, as a manager, on how to proceed when *Managing People*.

Wittily illustrated by Paula Youens' cartoons.

# NOTES

# NOTES

Angela Mcfarlane